Life in Revolutionary France

(Overleaf) The Fall of the Bastille — symbol of the overthrow of despotism

LIFE IN
REVOLUTIONARY FRANCE

Gwynne Lewis

European Life Series
Edited by Peter Quennell

London: B T BATSFORD LTD
New York: G P PUTNAM'S SONS

914.4
L674L

To my parents

First published 1972
© Gwynne Lewis 1972

Made and printed in Great Britain
by Jarrold & Sons Ltd, Norwich, Norfolk.
for the publishers
B. T. BATSFORD LTD
4 Fitzhardinge Street, London W.1
G. P. PUTNAM'S SONS
200 Madison Avenue, New York, N.Y. 10016

7134 1556 8

Contents

30196

Author's Acknowledgments

Are due in the first place to Richard Cobb, not for any direct assistance with this book, but for his invaluable guidance and stimulus over the years. Also to Roger Magraw and Michael Shepherd my colleagues at Warwick—but chiefly to the pioneers of the social history of the Revolution, Georges Lefebvre, George Rudé and Albert Sobeul.

The author and publishers wish to thank the following for permission to reproduce the illustrations appearing in this book:
Bibliothèque Nationale for numbers 5, 8–14, 16, 18, 19, 27, 30–32, 34–36, 39, 40, 42, 45, 49, 55–57, 60, 61, 63, 65, 66, 70–72, 75, 77, 79 and 80; M. Bidault de l'Isle for numbers 28, 33, 41, 43, 46, 52, 58 and 68; the Trustees of the British Museum for numbers 17, 29, 44, 48, 64, 67, 69 and 74; J. E. Bulloz, Paris, for the Frontispiece and numbers 47, 51, 53, 59, 62, 73 and 76; the Mansell Collection for numbers 4, 6, 37, 38, 54 and 78; the Musée Carnavalet and J. E. Bulloz for the jacket illustration; the Radio Times Hulton Picture Library for numbers 1–3, 7, 15, 20–26 and 50.

List of Illustrations

The jacket illustration is taken from the painting 'le Depart des Conscrits de 1807' by L. L. Boilly.

**The 83 Departments
of France, 1790**
(excluding Corsica)

THE AUSTRIAN

NETHERLANDS

THE EMPIRE

SWITZERLAND

SAVOY

ISÈRE

NICE

SPAIN

PAS DE CALAIS

NORD

SOMME

SEINE INFÉRIEURE

MANCHE

CALVADOS

ORNE

EURE

OISE

AISNE

ARDENNES

MEUSE

MOSELLE

MEURTHE

FINISTÈRE

CÔTES-DU-NORD

ILLE ET VILAINE

MORBIHAN

MAYENNE

SARTHE

EURE ET LOIR

PARIS

SEINE ET OISE

SEINE ET MARNE

MARNE

AUBE

HAUTE-MARNE

VOSGES

HAUT-RHIN

BAS-RHIN

LOIRE INFÉRIEURE

MAINE-ET-LOIRE

INDRE-ET-LOIRE

LOIR-ET-CHER

LOIRET

YONNE

CÔTE-D'OR

HAUTE-SAÔNE

VENDÉE

DEUX SÈVRES

VIENNE

INDRE

CHER

NIÈVRE

SAÔNE-ET-LOIRE

DOUBS

JURA

CHARENTE INFÉRIEURE

CHARENTE

HAUTE-VIENNE

CREUSE

ALLIER

PUY-DE-DÔME

RHÔNE ET LOIRE

AIN

CORRÈZE

DORDOGNE

CANTAL

HAUTE-LOIRE

ARDÈCHE

DRÔME

HAUTES-ALPES

GIRONDE

LOT-ET-GARONNE

LOT

AVEYRON

LOZÈRE

GARD

AVIGNON VENAISSIN

BASSES-ALPES

BOUCHES-DU-RHÔNE

VAR

LANDES

GERS

TARN

HÉRAULT

BASSES-PYRÉNÉES

HAUTES-PYRÉNÉES

HAUTE-GARONNE

ARIÈGE

AUDE

PYRÉNÉES ORIENTALES

N

Paris became the Department
of the Seine; Rhône-et-Loire
was divided into Rhône and
Loire, as two Departments.
As a result of the first annexations,
Mont-Blanc—i.e. Savoie and Haute-Savoie—
came from Savoy; Alpes-Maritimes from Nice and
Monaco; Mont-Terrible—i.e. Territory-de-Belfort—
from the district of Porentruy; and Vaucluse from Avignon
and the Comtat-Venaissin. By 1799 there were 90 départements in all.

*The Revolution created an administrative structure which has lasted
to the present day.*

Introduction

France in 1789 was governed, in theory, by an Absolute Monarch, a Catholic Church which claimed spiritual sovereignty over the lives of all Frenchmen (conveniently ignoring the existence of a large Protestant minority) and a feudal order which subjugated the peasantry, economically and juridically, to an aristocratic class. In fact, the king, Louis XVI, was not absolute enough to control even his own Court, the Church had lost, or was in the process of losing, its hold over a large section of the population, and it was the vestiges rather than the reality of feudalism which vexed the peasantry. It was the widening gulf between the theory and practice of *ancien régime* government and society which made it so difficult to construct any permanent bridges of reform.

From many points of view, French society in 1789 was still fairly static. For the vast majority of Frenchmen, the daily routine continued to be governed by the unfolding of the seasons and the calendar of the Church. The Church was recognised in the hierarchy of the *ancien régime* as the First Estate of the realm, the aristocracy forming the Second Estate and the remaining ninety-five per cent of the population the Third Estate. Four Frenchmen in every five were engaged in, or associated with, some form of agricultural labour. Neither the methods of tilling the soil nor the techniques of producing manufactured goods had altered dramatically since the sixteenth century. The ships which brought so much wealth to France from her colonies were still propelled by the winds above the surface of the earth rather than the coal hewn from beneath it. To find large factories at the end of the eighteenth century was difficult; to discover machines driven by steam-power was almost impossible. One cannot speak of the existence of a factory proletariat. The labour-force of Paris and the larger provincial cities was still dominated by the thousands of small-scale craftsmen, shop-keepers and workers, male and female, who serviced the wasteful and cumbersome economic machinery of *ancien régime* France. Medieval man, granted divine dispensation to pay a fleeting visit to France in the 1780s, would have been far less astonished to witness the changes in the production and distribution of goods than revolutionary man performing the same function just sixty or seventy years later.

This static aspect of the *ancien régime* was more accurately reflected in its government than in its society. Louis XVI, who had ascended the throne in 1774, was a popular but none too gifted Monarch. Inheriting a system which enabled Ministers to pursue their own independent and frequently contradictory policies, Louis soon decided that it would be wiser not to involve himself too deeply in the decision-making process. He was concerned, however, that the person, rather than the policies, of the Monarchy should continue to be respected.

Lacking central direction, the Monarchy was also weakened by a multiplicity of traditional restraints. The thirteen *parlements* of the realm, spearheaded by the *parlement* of Paris, which claimed the right of registering royal edicts, formed the most effective opposition lobby. These sovereign courts, although composed in the main of ennobled magistrates who had turned their offices into hereditary seats of privilege, successfully projected an image of themselves as protectors of the people's liberties. *Parlements*, provincial estates, the assemblies of the Church, municipalities, guilds and corporations further restricted the power of the Crown. It can be argued with some confidence that the French Monarchy fell in 1789 not because it was too absolute but because it was not absolute enough.

If one enquires more deeply, however, it soon becomes evident that France in the eighteenth century was experiencing radical change. The most obvious change was that there were many more Frenchmen in 1789 than there had been in 1700, an increase in fact of well over twenty per cent. This marked rise in population created acute social and economic dislocation: a more intense struggle for land; greater strain on food reserves; problems of public order and administration for the government; increased poverty producing more beggars which in turn provoked more violence in the countryside and the towns.

Although France did not undergo a *technological* revolution, trade and industry expanded at a rate which compared favourably with that of her closest rival, Great Britain: her colonial trade, in particular, was flourishing. The increased volume of wealth tapped from the more remunerative sectors of the economy was eagerly exploited by the middle classes, and just as eagerly translated into privilege. There were very few posts under the *ancien régime* which could not be bought for the right price. The colour of one's money was almost as important as the colour of one's blood during the eighteenth century. It was widely accepted, of course, that only Bourbon blood qualified one to sit on the throne of France and that, normally, a strain of blue blood was desirable for an Archbishop or an Admiral; further down the religious, military or administrative hierarchy, however, offices were often sold to the highest bidder.

One can exaggerate, therefore, the extent to which the Revolution created a close relationship between wealth and political power. The apparent obsession of the revolutionary with the all-pervasive and corrupting influence of wealth can only be explained by its increasing importance during the *ancien régime*. If it could not always buy political power, it granted the well-to-do social status and the arrogance which attended it. The course of the Revolution was to be dictated, to some degree, by men who felt that their education and talents qualified them for more than an obscure existence behind some desk or lectern in a sleepy, provincial town; men whose intellectual and social pre-tensions were weightier than their wallets. Robespierre's vision of a society of small-owners and producers—shared by thousands of petty Robespierres—had been conjured up whilst he was suffering the vexations of a small-town lawyer in Arras.

Again, although it is true that at the popular level men's minds were still conditioned by the dictates of a Divine Monarch, the Catholic Church, and the vagaries of the climate, shafts of light had begun to penetrate the gloom. The *Encyclopédie*, first published in the 1750s, contained the corporate wisdom of radical thinkers like Rousseau, Voltaire, Diderot and Montesquieu. Rousseau propagated dangerous ideas such as the 'sovereignty of the people' and the concept of a 'general will'; Voltaire's vitriolic pen created an image of the Church as cruel, intolerant and superstitious. Renewed impetus to the spread of liberal ideas came from across the Atlantic, a consequence of French involve-ment in the American War of Independence. The writers and thinkers of the late eighteenth century did not make, indeed did not want, a revolution, but they did provide the intellectual ammunition for one.

The changes outlined above clearly affected urban centres more immediately than the countryside. From this point of view, an individual response to the Revolution was often determined by geography rather than social status. A petty noble farming a tiny estate in Brittany had little in common with a courtier at Versailles: a wealthy aristocrat living in Toulouse, engaged in a lucrative commercial or speculative venture, differed in his attitude from both. A bourgeois inhabiting a small parliamentary town such as Rennes was not likely to share an identity of interest with a manufacturer of luxury goods in Paris: a wealthy farmer from the Beauce region was again confronted with very different problems. The Revolution was to sharpen the growing antagonism between the town and the countryside. Owing to the absence of modern forms of communication—even the Press was in its infancy—new ideas took much longer to radiate outwards from urban centres. The time-lag involved in the dissemination of such ideas was to have important consequences after 1789, for, in general, the Revolution spread in shock-waves from Paris to the provincial cities and towns and then finally, often encountering bitter resistance, to the countryside.

No section of the French community, social or institutional, was able to immunise itself against the virus of change. The Church reflected within its ranks that same division between wealth and poverty which characterised society as a whole. The aristocratic style of life adopted by most archbishops, bishops and abbots alienated the lower orders of the clergy who tended to identify themselves, at least at a material level, with their poor parishioners. This fundamental split within the Church was to be of great significance in the political events of 1789.

The aristocracy was to enter the fray in an even more divided condition. A small group of liberal nobles, resenting the exclusion of the aristocracy from the corridors of power, actually began the long process of political debate which was to end with the collapse of the Monarchy; others were content to extract more revenues from their estates; a few, particularly courtiers at Versailles, were satisfied with the system of outdoor relief provided by the Court in the form of pensions, sinecures and outright gifts. The struggle in 1789 was not a straightforward one between the clergy and the nobility on the one hand and the Third Estate on the other; it was more a coalition of dissenting elements from within each separate Estate, although, increasingly, the bourgeoisie tended to play a leading role.

By this time, the Monarchy had proved to be bankrupt not only in ideas but also in terms of hard cash. The incredibly wasteful system of taxation upon which the Government depended for its revenues, aggravated by the cost of involvement in the American War of Independence, had completely exhausted its financial reserves. It was decided, in 1787, to convoke an Assembly of Notables to sanction yet another programme of reform. The selfish interests of the nobility, represented in particular by the *parlements*, created a constitutional impasse between the Court and the Country which was finally resolved by the convocation of an Estates General. Such a body had not met in France for over 150 years. The basic changes in the society and economy of France since the seventeenth century ensured that its response to the demands of the Court would be far less docile. The harvest failures of 1787-88, bringing in their wake a serious slump in the manufacturing sector of the economy, produced that explosive conjunction of circumstances which transformed a constitutional crisis into a revolution.

The impact of the Revolution was to be felt, in varying degrees, not only in France or even in Europe, but throughout the western world. Many contemporaries felt with Wordsworth that, 'Bliss was it in that dawn to be alive'; others, like Joseph de Maistre, were convinced that Hell itself had unleashed a pack of devils to chastise the French for their ungodliness. But, consciously or unconsciously, everyone was to be affected in some way by the Revolution. It is with the reaction of different sections of the French community to this historic event that this book is principally concerned.

I The Decline of an Aristocratic Society

French society on the eve of the Revolution was dominated by the aristocracy. From the remotest provincial village to Versailles itself the cultural, social, economic and administrative life of France was profoundly affected by aristocratic values and interests. It would be totally misleading to suggest that the Revolution completely destroyed this influence: traces of it persist to the present day. During the Napoleonic period, and particularly under the Bourbon Restoration which followed in 1814, the aristocracy were to regain a great deal of their former importance, a task facilitated by the eagerness of the middle classes to ape—as they had been taught to do in the seventeenth and eighteenth centuries—the manners and customs of their 'superiors'. However, it remains true that by 1814 French society had been fundamentally altered by the Revolution; so indeed had the composition and character of the aristocracy.

In the pyramid of power which had the monarch as its apex, the French nobility formed the Second Estate of the realm, the clergy representing the First and the mass of the population the Third Estate. In practice, the nobility dominated life at Court and controlled the key positions in the Church and the army. They numbered about 350,000, less than two per cent of the total population of France, and were to be found in greater concentration in the North and West than in the Centre and the South-East. Most of the land was divided into seigneuries, comprising the *domaine directe* which the lord cultivated himself or leased out to tenants and the *domaine utile* over which the lord continued to exercise certain specific rights. In the West, the nobility might own over sixty per cent of the land; in parts of the South-East the percentage dropped to ten or less. They did not represent a 'class' in the modern sense of the term, nor even a cohesive social group. There was little identity of interest between a wealthy courtier at Versailles and a Breton or Languedoc seigneur grubbing out a meagre livelihood, 'often so poor that he ploughs his own fields'. But, whether rich or poor, the great majority of nobles were fiercely proud of their rights and privileges. A French noble may not have had a *sou* in his pocket but the right to wear a sword in his belt marked him out as one of the élite. In a society where practically everyone could claim some privilege or other, the aristocracy were more privileged than most.

The true 'aristocrat' who could (and usually did) trace his ancestry back, if not to the Frankish invaders of Gaul, then at least to the Middle Ages, was a very rare phenomenon, a small minority of the nobility. Those presented at Court numbered no more than 4,000. Endebted to a degree that only the luxury of living amidst great wealth can explain, the Court nobility were not particularly moral, religious, or politically useful, all of which did not prevent them from monopolising the positions of archbishops, bishops, generals, admirals or ministers of the Crown. Contrary to what one might expect they were not slow to supplement their incomes by taking an interest in commerce and industry. Nobles were to be found as mine-owners, grain speculators, money-lenders and even wholesale traders (dabbling in the retail business, however, would have involved loss of noble status). The Marshal de Castries, the last Minister of the Marine under Louis XVI,

I   *A seigneur's wife deals with tradesmen while completing her morning toilette*

had important mining interests in Languedoc; the duc d'Orleans, a prince of the blood, apart from owning vast property in Paris and the provinces, had invested considerable funds in speculative, financial, commercial and building ventures of the 1780s.

It is true that the Bourbon kings, pressing forward with their programme of centralisation, had destroyed much of the political power and regional influence of the old nobility, preferring to rely on middle-class support. But this policy had only led to the creation of a new noble caste—the nobility of the robe. The more important offices in the administration, the judiciary and the army conferred noble status of varying degrees upon the purchaser. Long after the need for loyal civil servants had passed, the need for money had obliged the Bourbons to fabricate offices and titles of nobility for the deserving bourgeoisie. One could become Secretary to the King for 5,000 livres—Louis XVI had 800 of them! Or one could buy a regiment in the army, although, since there were never enough regiments to go around, it was necessary to rotate the command with two or three other candidates. In the course of the eighteenth century the *noblesse de robe* invaded every public and private domain of the old nobility, buying up their estates, entering their salons, marrying their daughters, encroaching upon their preserves in the Church. Noble escutcheons were being blotted, not by wayward sons, but by frequent intermarriage, as the crustier members of the caste were constantly pointing out.

There were many municipal offices which also elevated the purchaser into the ranks of the nobility, although the so-called *noblesse de cloche* could not usually transmit their titles to their heirs. Such men would have felt honoured to have been invited to the local seigneur's ball to say nothing of the giddy heights of being presented at Versailles. Little wonder that to the foreigner the French nobility was something of an enigma, a patchwork quilt of privilege and prejudice.

Jealousy and personal animosity naturally flourished within a caste which placed so much emphasis on snobbery. Apart from the hopeless struggle of the old nobility against the pretensions of the new, there was a basic rift between the Court and the provincial nobility. The comte de Lubersac, presenting an unconvincing defence of his order, admitted that 'some nobles deserve criticism, but not all. One has to distinguish between the Court and the provincial nobility . . . the latter are the

2 *A salon during the reign of Louis XVI*

friends of the peasantry for whom they provide work and with whom they share both good times and bad.' In the Auvergne, noble incomes of less than 600 livres a year were not uncommon; in Brittany, Arthur Young, the English agronomist whose *Journal* provides so much valuable information on the state of France in 1789, writes that he found many of the nobles extremely poor but tenacious of their rights, commenting in particular on one 'Bas Breton noble with his sword and a little miserable but nimble nag.'

Strongly attached to local customs, living often in dilapidated and draughty chateaux, adversely affected by the price-rise of the eighteenth century, posts in the army, the Church and the administration harder to come by at a time when money rather than birth secured advancement, little wonder that the provincial nobility tended to be more anarchist than aristocratic. Many a provincial noble, like the comte d'Antraigues in the Vivarais, who rushed to defend the Monarchy and the Church during the Revolution, had exhibited a similar degree of enthusiasm for attacking both institutions before 1789.

For by no means all the members of the nobility were reactionary. Indeed the aristocrat's political bible in the eighteenth century was Montesquieu's *Esprit des lois,* not only on account of its liberal senti-

3　*Louis XVI arriving at the Hotel de Ville three days*
after the fall of the Bastille

ments, but because it also provided a theoretical justification for
an attack on royal absolutism. The nobility had its complement of
'intellectuals', from the rich and influential duc de Liancourt to the
dissolute but imposing figure of Mirabeau. The marquis de Lafayette
had discovered his liberal leanings while fighting against the British
in the American War of Independence. Well-represented in the
parlements and provincial estates, which acted as a brake on royal power,
the nobility in the eighteenth century were engaged in a struggle with the
Crown for political power. It was their criticism, articulated in the
Assembly of Notables in 1787, of the Court's handling of the political
and financial crisis which first produced a revolutionary situation in
France. Their brief flirtation with such dangerous concepts as liberty
and freedom, however, was to cost a few of them their heads, many more

their property and, as an élite, their undisputed pre-eminence in society.

The first blow fell on the night of 4th August 1789 when the recently-formed National Assembly, composed of the Third and the more liberal members of the first two Estates, decreed the 'abolition of feudalism', a term which confused contemporaries almost as much as present-day historians. Juridically 'feudalism' had lost much of its meaning, but the peasants (who knew more about it than anyone else) still felt it to be relevant to their daily lives. The economic rewards of the system, so far as the nobility were concerned, varied according to local custom. The majority of peasants, although they regarded themselves as property-owners, still paid certain dues in money or kind, the *cens* or the *champart*, in recognition of their subservience to the seigneur. In addition there were payments to be made when a peasant bought or sold land, the *lods et ventes*; grain had to be ground into flour at the lord's mill; bread had to be baked in his ovens and grapes turned into wine by using his press. In some areas, like Poitou and the Auvergne, the peasant could not sell his wine until the lord had first been given an opportunity of cornering the market.

There was, in fact, from one region to another, a bewildering variety of dues, rents, forced labour contracts which provided employment for a small army of legal experts who were heartily disliked by the peasantry. Many peasants were prepared, grudgingly, to keep to these contracts; the vast majority, however, resented the lord's exclusive right to hunt, fish, and keep pigeons which wreaked havoc on their crops. To ensure that the system continued to operate in the best interests of the seigneur there were manorial courts, controlled by the lord himself, which settled litigation between tenants and landlords.

Throughout the latter part of the century many seigneùrs had been busily rewriting old charters and contracts in order to squeeze more money and produce from their tenants. In some regions, the bourgeoisie, having purchased seigneurial estates, had introduced managers to run the estate more efficiently and at a greater profit: the bourgeois often proved to be a more exacting landlord than the old seigneur. Noble or bourgeois attempting to 'live nobly', the distinction was lost on the peasant.

During the summer of 1789, provoked beyond measure by such exactions, suffering acutely from the bad harvests of 1787 and 1788,

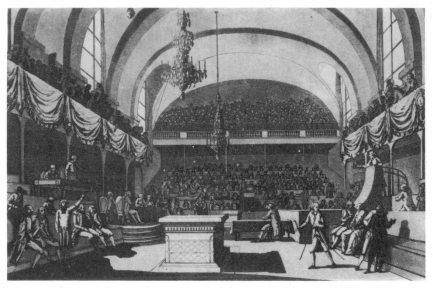

4   *After 9 November 1789, the National Assembly, seen here in
session, met in a room formerly used as a riding school*

and having some obscure understanding of the political crisis as a result
of which 'something was to be done by some great folk for the likes of
us', the peasants indulged in one of their periodic bouts of collective
violence. Hence the 'abolition of feudalism' was not exactly an act of
altruism on the part of the middle-class deputies; it was to some extent
imposed upon them by the *Grande Peur*, the remarkable spasm of
violence and panic in the French countryside, directed principally
against the aristocracy. Arthur Young, passing through Besançon on
27 July found 'the mischiefs which have been perpetrated . . . numerous and shocking. Many chateaux have been burnt, others plundered,
the seigneurs hunted down like wild beasts, their wives and daughters
ravished, their papers and titles burnt and all their property destroyed.'

The aristocracy might well have survived the consequences of 4
August; politicians rarely mean what they say and the peasantry soon
discovered that the old system was not to be destroyed but merely
modified. It was only as a result of the war and their bitter resistance to
the continued payment of dues that the peasantry were to be truly
emancipated. This decision, taken in 1793, to abolish all remaining

vestiges of the feudal regime entailed, in many cases, unjustifiable hardship for the nobility.

However, not all seigneurs suffered alike. In the region around Toulouse and Bordeaux the loss of feudal dues represented less than a ten per cent drop in income for the nobility. In other areas, where a more traditional pattern of life existed, it proved to be as high as sixty per cent. On the duc d'Orleans property in the Gatinais no less than two-thirds of the annual income came from feudal dues. But one cannot measure the blow inflicted simply in percentages; in many instances the noble's pride was affected more deeply than his pocket. Along with feudal dues the noble lost his privileged position in society. He no longer dispensed justice on the manor; henceforth he was to be judged by the same yardstick as any other mortal. He lost his exclusive hunting and fishing rights; he no longer marched at the head of local processions or saw the village church draped in mourning when a member of his family died. But laws do not immediately change habits and customs developed over centuries; life in the French countryside particularly in the remoter regions, did not change overnight. Some examples have been found of feudal dues being paid throughout the Revolution and it was a bold peasant who dared to sit in the pew traditionally reserved for the seigneur.

Nevertheless, as the Revolution became progressively more radical so life for the noble became increasingly difficult. In June 1791 the Royal Family had bungled their attempt to escape from France and the Revolution. The flight, abortive as it was, had destroyed any real possibility of an alliance between the Court and the National Assembly. Louis XVI, a kindly, but indolent and ineffectual monarch, continually harassed by an unstable wife and a factious Court, found himself drifting along with the tide of events that were to lead, for him and Marie Antoinette, to the guillotine. The outbreak of war in April 1792 evoked a tremendous patriotic response from the French people that was to be focussed, for the first time in its history, not on the Monarch but the National Assembly. The storming of the Tuileries on 10 August by the Parisian crowd and the creation of a Republic one month later signalled the end of Absolute Monarchy in France. Many nobles decided to set out on the journey which, for some, was to mean over twenty years of hardship and suffering.

6　*The Royal Family three days after the execution of Louis XVI*

Many of the king's closest relatives, including the comte d'Artois
and the comte de Provence, had emigrated after the fall of the Bastille
in July 1789; hundreds of nobles, with their families and what servants
they could afford, had followed in their footsteps during the next two
years. It was more than a duty; it was the fashion. As the comte des
Echerolles explained: 'It was difficult to stand against the prevailing
current of opinion which, resting on the concept of honour, became an
imperative for us'.

With the seizure of power by the Jacobins in 1793 the situation
became far more desperate. Although the lurid and romantic tales of
Dickens and Baroness d'Orczy offer a very distorted image of life for
the aristocracy, their situation during the period known as the Terror—
from the summer of 1793 to that of the following year—was hardly an
enviable one. In the capital, and the main centres of counter-revolutionary agitation, the shadow of the guillotine fell on many nobles crowded
into the prisons. Madame des Echerolles provides us with an account

5　*A royalist depiction of the execution of Louis XVI.*
　　Note the displeasure of the Heavens!

of the suffering of her aunt, a victim of the severe repression in Lyons at the end of 1793. Shunted from prison to prison she was eventually condemned to death. Madame des Echerolles, a witness of these events, records how the prisoners 'listened in profound silence to the reading of the death sentences and then, with the same serenity, walked from the Town Hall to the place of execution where a priest was waiting to give his blessing. My aunt was the first to climb the steps of the guillotine'.

But not every aristocrat spent his days during the Terror hiding in attics or ditches from the brutal and vindictive members of the local *comité révolutionnaire*. Some nobles, like the comte d'Antraigues, even confessed a sneaking admiration for the Jacobins: they might at the very least (always supposing someone was prepared to act on his latest master-plan for counter-revolution) provoke anarchy and thus facilitate the return of a Monarch who would place himself in the hands of the aristocracy. The majority of the nobility, provided they dropped their titles and reconciled themselves to living in semi-obscurity (inviting the president of the local Popular Society to tea was a shrewd method of survival), were allowed to exist in a sort of political and social vacuum. The Chasteneys went to Rouen, rented a small apartment, and spent most of their time reading or playing chess. Servants and friends could often be relied upon in times of crisis and bribery was not unknown even in the days of the virtuous Robespierre. Less than ten per cent of

7   *Search of a royalist household during the Terror*

the nobility went into exile, affecting, it has been suggested, 'about one noble family in four'. An even smaller percentage of the nobility physically lost their heads.

Nor should it be supposed that the nobility were deprived of all, or even the greater part, of their property. Expropriation laws were passed against émigrés not against nobles who elected to remain in France, and even the émigrés managed to recover much of their property under Napoleon and the Bourbon Restoration. In the department of the Sarthe, the nobility lost about 100,000 acres as a result of the Revolution; by 1830 practically all this land had been restored to its former owners. No doubt exceptional, but the relatives, friends and agents of those in exile did succeed in saving a great deal. Professor Robert Forster, in an admittedly rough guess, suggests that the provincial nobility lost about one-fifth of their land and a third of their income. This—if correct—represents an appreciable loss, but by no means a general disaster.

For those who made the decision to leave France—often prompted to do so by poison-pen letters from a local countess—the early crusading spirit degenerated into a daily struggle for survival. Despite the common suffering the old snobbery within the ranks of the nobility was, if anything, more noticeable in exile than it had been in France. At Coblentz, where the comte d'Artois held court, a miniature replica of Versailles was created where etiquette, complete to the last curtsey, was rigorously observed. In London, the richer émigrés frequented the fashionable areas of the West End, especially Marylebone; the poorer went to Southwark or Soho eking out a fairly miserable existence despite a gift of £40 'from the young gentlemen of Harrow'. The famous author, Chateaubriand, tells us in his memoirs that he once walked the streets of London sucking a piece of cloth dipped in water to assuage the pangs of hunger; the de Lamasc family emigrated to Germany where one brother earned just enough to pay his lodgings by giving lessons in French while his mother and his sister embroidered cloth which was sold at the local market. One could find French émigrés making a living out of money-changing in Hamburg, serving behind bars or even selling second-hand clothes in Coblentz.

Life in the émigré battalions which were formed to overthrow the godless Revolution often proved to be even more miserable, although here at least the émigré could console himself with the thought that he was serving in his traditional capacity as a soldier. Pay was often months in arrears; those in the lower ranks were badly equipped and ragged in appearance. The marquis de Touslain was once overheard bemoaning the fact that his regiment 'looked more like a brigand's reunion than a detachment of soldiers'. Even the great Condé's army was eventually to suffer the indignity of becoming mercenaries for other European rulers. If one were captured by Republican troops one could expect little mercy: after the failure of the Quiberon expedition to the west coast of France in 1795—an expedition which was finally to destroy any illusions the émigrés still held about overthrowing the Republic by force of arms—700 prisoners were captured and shot, over half of the number being of noble birth. The comte d'Artois, who was always threatening to lead an expedition, successfully avoided this one.

The onslaught upon the aristocracy also affected the lives of thousands of ordinary Frenchmen who were drawn socially or economically within their orbit. As France presided over the birth of a new egalitarian society all the paraphenalia of an aristocratic age was swept away. A member of the Popular Society of Tarbes explained what this meant to a visitor: 'You will have to look hard for aristocratic hair-styles here, or for those flowery and flowering cravats and we don't have much perfumed rose-water . . . our language is as simple as our dress', all of which meant disaster for a horde of wig-makers, hair-dressers, jewellers, coachmakers and goldsmiths, to say nothing of the tens of thousands of servants, only a minority of whom could follow their masters and mistresses into exile and who were often boycotted by Popular Societies as carriers of the dreaded aristocratic plague. Artists suffered as patrons disappeared; theatre managers were forced to change their repertoires; gaming-houses closed their doors (although not for long). The repercussions of the anti-aristocratic crusade were varied and, for some, extremely painful.

The execution of Robespierre and his supporters in the summer of 1794 marked the end of the political and economic system known as the Terror. It also released the social restraints which had been placed on people's lives. From the aristocracy and counter-revolutionaries in general there was a widespread call for revenge. Revenge in the first instance on the dour, repressive and colourless daily life of previous

8 *'The victim's shirt': a sartorial mockery of the Terror with its exaggerated neck-line*

years: sensuality replaced Jacobin morality as the *leitmotiv* of the age. Affected, garish, and vulgar it may have been, but at least, according to the privileged who lived through those dying years of the eighteenth century, it was great fun. People flocked to the theatres; gaming-houses and salons reappeared; couples danced in the Carmes prison where only a few years earlier the blood of priests massacred by the Parisian crowd had flowed. The uninhibited styles of dress reflected the overthrow of restraint and convention. The ladies sallied forth in their dresses which revealed far more of their feminine charms than either the weather or propriety advised. Royalist youth decked itself in its finest apparel before setting out to beat up workers and former terrorists in the streets—the *jeunesse dorée* 'with their cravats, yellow or black collars, white gloves and buttons fashioned in the form of the *fleur-de-lys*'. It became the fashion for guests to arrive at balls with their necks shaved, as if in preparation for the guillotine, and thin red silk bands around their throats—a macabre mockery of the Terror.

For those on the receiving end of this reaction to the Terror life was not at all funny. The poor and the disinherited suffered more acutely, particularly during and after the terrible winter of 1795, than at any time during the Revolution. In Paris and the provinces a 'White Terror', initiated and executed by the Royalists, claimed an impressive number of victims. In the West and the South-East the desire to revenge a father or brother murdered during the Revolution dovetailed quite neatly into the long tradition of rural crime and brigandage. Royalist gangs exacted a terrible vengeance in and around the city of Lyons; there were prison massacres in Nimes, Arles, Avignon and Marseilles. Richard Cobb has estimated that 'eight hundred persons of both sexes were murdered' in the South-East between 1795 and 1800. Certainly the nobility as such played only a minor role in these massacres, but it is evident that after 1795 Royalism became increasingly popular, a popularity reflected in the Jacobin press which, in Lyons, denounced the activities of bands of youths killing good Republicans in the streets while 'in the doors and windows of their fine houses, women, dressed in the latest fashion and wearing Royalist brooches, applauded loudly'. It is difficult to escape the conclusion that there was a certain class bias in the activities of these bands.

The relaxation of much of the legislation directed against émigrés, coupled with the more favourable climate of public opinion, encouraged many nobles either to return from abroad or to re-emerge from hiding. There was an air of confidence that, with the end of the Terror, the bout of madness which had seized France was over and that the nobility could now reassert something of their former authority. It was still necessary to be extremely careful: there were powerful factions in the government, in the army and in society at large which resisted strongly any notion of a return to the old order. The elections of 1797, which returned a Royalist majority, provoked those in power to annul the elections and to launch a renewed campaign against nobles and priests. Once again, the game of 'hunt the aristocrat' was declared legal. One countess, sheltered by a friend in his daughter's room, was warned 'not to open the shutters, not to light a fire or a lamp. I shall try to bring you some cold food, but only once a day. Try not to walk around too heavily since the apartment beneath is occupied.'

A great deal depended on the attitude of the local authorities, particularly in the absence by 1799 of any effective central government. Forged documents could be presented to show that a noble, placed on the lists of émigrés drawn up in 1793, had never really left France and could therefore reclaim his property. In areas like Normandy, the nobility repossessed a considerable amount of property before the rise to power of Napoleon Bonaparte. A speech made in the *Conseil des Anciens*—one of the two Legislative organs of the Directory—went so far as to express the opinion that 'a former noble, who has contributed to the cause of the Revolution, who has honoured himself by wearing the colours of liberty in some public office, should receive the rewards due to him'.

It was, therefore, during the Directory, from 1795 to 1799, that the aristocracy began the painful process of readjusting to the political and social realities of post-revolutionary France. This process was accelerated after the *coup d'état* of November 1799 which brought Napoleon Bonaparte to power. If Bonaparte had not existed, it would have been necessary to invent him. The disintegration of the political, social and economic life of France made the restoration of 'law and order' an absolute necessity. Seven years of war and revolution had produced a widespread feeling of apathy and weariness. For many, Napoleon seemed to offer the best chance of securing a lasting peace, the first, but not the last time that a General was chosen to end a war. For a brief period, notably as a result of the Peace of Amiens in 1801, Napoleon gave the French what they wanted—peace and reconstruction. The remainder of his reign was to be dedicated to the pursuit of military glory.

Despite the debt which Napoleon owed to the Revolution, a debt which is clearly evident in his religious, legal, economic and adminstrative reforms, his personal sympathies lay with the Enlightened Despots of the *ancien régime*. Authority, order and discipline were to be the materials from which Napoleon constructed his Imperial edifice; the aristocracy was to provide the outer façade. The son of a petty Corsican noble, Napoleon always displayed a certain predilection for the aristocracy; not that he wished to recreate in its entirety the hierarch-

9　*The coronation of Napoleon Bonaparte*

ical structure of the Absolute Monarchy. It was simply that just as religion was good for the masses so an aristocracy would be useful in creating the Empire which was announced in 1804. Already, hundreds of émigrés had returned to France justifiably suspicious of Napoleon's intentions but convinced that the worst excesses of the Revolution were over. They returned to a country which still bore the marks of a decade of violent change. How would they integrate into the new social order?

Napoleon himself tried hard to create the necessary environment: 'A newly-born government', he told his secretary, 'must dazzle and astonish.' At Court he introduced the ceremony and etiquette of Versailles. Josephine was given a few ladies-in-waiting chosen from the families of the old nobility; a code was produced for Court procedure which contained no less than 819 articles; Napoleon even went hunting, not because he enjoyed the sport, but because it was the regal thing to do. An eminent member of the old nobility, Louis-Phillipe Ségur, was appointed to the Council of State, and many of Napoleon's Generals were 'advised' to marry the daughters of aristocrats. At the lavish dinner-parties and soirées held at the Tuileries the ladies appeared, on Napoleon's instructions, resplendent in dresses befitting those of an Imperial Court. Josephine set the fashion, particularly in her love of expensive jewellery. One necklace alone, made from a set of pearls which had belonged to Marie Antoinette, cost 250,000 francs, more than a skilled worker under the Empire might earn in a lifetime. Like Josephine's necklace, however, the Empire itself was 'second-hand'. Despite the magnificent balls and dinners, and the private theatrical productions at his home, Malmaison, Napoleon's Court, even after the Generals had been told to leave their uniforms at home, lacked grace and refinement. The Bourbon Court had conducted itself along the lines of a minuet; Napoleon's ran more like a military manoeuvre.

The attempt at reconciliation was only partially successful. Napoleon offered the nobility a more useful function than that which they had performed under the *ancien régime*, but service to an anointed Bourbon was one thing; to a petty Corsican upstart, quite another. Most of the old aristocracy kept their distance, congregating in the fashionable Faubourg Saint-Germain in Paris where the Trémoilles, the Fitz-James's and the Montmorencys organised resistance to the Emperor. Although in the Parisian and provincial salons the refined conversations of aristocratic tongues could be heard once again, the more uncompromising nobles maintained a strict policy of social apartheid. Certain salons, such as *chez* Madame de Reynière, were reserved for the aristocracy. A high-born Russian lady, Madame Divoff, commenting in her entertaining memoirs on the snobbery of these aristocratic circles, thought that the ladies had developed the art of elongating their noses to prove their long ancestry. 'It was', she writes of one hostess, 'as if she had deliberately invited to her house all the aristocratic ladies of Paris with long noses'.

In this exclusive, if somewhat unreal, world it was still birth not wealth which secured an entrée to society. The duchesse de Luynes's soirées 'were always crowded with people, but all former nobles. There were a few present who were so poor that they had been obliged to arrive on foot.' Under the Empire, the impoverished nobility, often hounded by creditors for debts incurred before the Revolution, developed their own form of genteel begging—for instance a card presented to the doorman, embossed with any noble coat-of-arms, could be relied upon to provide a free meal.

Since most of the old noble families betrayed a marked reluctance to accept Napoleon on his own terms he felt obliged to create an aristocracy of his own. He had already exploited the vacant thrones of Europe as a system of outdoor relief for his importunate family—Jerome, ruler of the newly-created 'Kingdom of Westphalia', Louis, King of Holland, Joseph, 'King of Spain and the Indies' and his sister Caroline as co-ruler of Naples and Sicily. In 1802, he had introduced the Légion d'Honneur as a means of rewarding his faithful followers (the fact that this honour is still much coveted by Frenchmen suggests how well Napoleon knew his subjects). His principal Ministers were given estates carved out of Italy. Having created kings and princes it was a small but logical step to fashion in March 1808 a new nobility, complete with dukes, counts, barons and imperial knights. Napoleon's crowning achievement, however, was his second marriage in 1809 to Marie Louise, the daughter of the Austrian Emperor. The 'little corporal' now felt that he was justified in referring to the future Louis XVIII as 'mon oncle'.

Thus, as a result of Napoleon's reign, the old nobility not only had to contend with the challenge of the bourgeoisie, but the creation of a rival caste. Successive French régimes have produced new political parties; Napoleon's régime was the only one to produce a new social group. There is also evidence that the behaviour of the old nobility was undergoing radical change. The de Lamasc family had returned in 1801 after eight years in exile totally disorientated by their past experiences and their future prospects. Their property had largely disappeared in the general *sauve qui peut*, divided 'between share-croppers, the petite bourgeoisie and a few former nobles who had joined with these brigands and profited at our expense'. Apparently there was more honour among thieves during the Revolution than among the aristocracy. Pradel de Lamasc himself was obliged to plunge into the murky waters of commerce in order to survive, his comment on this fall from aristocratic grace reflecting rather poignantly the mentality of the noble confronted by changing circumstances: 'I do not have any prejudice against merchants, but I consider that a gentleman, before entering upon such a career . . . must wait until all other doors are closed to him.'

Unfortunately for such families the Revolution had closed many doors to the aristocracy, and although the more influential and wealthy did succeed in recreating something of the style of life which had typified aristocratic society under the *ancien régime,* the majority were obliged to integrate more fully, if not totally, into the new society. The Revolution had not brought liberty in its wake, but it had introduced a measure of equality which made the reintroduction of the nobility as a ruling caste unrealistic. The Napoleonic Code had restricted the amount of property which a father could bequeath to the eldest son with the result that after 1815 many nobles were imitating the middle classes in dividing their property equally amongst all their children, further fragmenting the big noble estates. During the nineteenth century, the nobility, deprived of the privilege which had been legally and socially enforceable under the *ancien régime,* would have to rely on the paternalistic image to counter that of the philistine, grasping bourgeoisie immortalised in the novels of Balzac.

In 1814, Louis XVIII left Britain after a far warmer send-off by the City of London than he was to receive from his fellow-countrymen. Also included 'in the baggage-train of the Allies' was a small but vociferous group of émigrés who had never reconciled themselves even to the Napoleonic régime. The brief but disastrous return of Napoleon in the summer of 1815 enabled many of them to impose a more extreme form of Catholic Royalism upon the Monarchy. Gone was the frivolous, godless aristocracy of *ancien régime* France; in its place was a spiritually and politically regenerated caste. The next fifteen years were to present the Indian summer of the French aristocracy: it was to be the Revolution of 1830 which finally drove them, at least from a political point of view, into the cold.

2 Religion and Revolution

If France was an aristocratic society on the eve of the Revolution it was also profoundly Catholic: 'the eighteenth century was built upon religious foundations and even atheists could conceive of it with no other'. The Church, with its 200,000 regular and secular members, governed by an Assembly of high ecclesiastics, represented the First Order in the realm. Today it is possible for one to be born, to be educated, to be married, to live one's allotted span and to die, without being too aware of the presence of the Church. It was inconceivable in 1789. The Church kept the registers of births, deaths and marriages; it monopolised primary and secondary education; it was the major source of charity; it ran the hopelessly inadequate hospital service provided under the *ancien régime*. It escaped practically all forms of taxation, voting instead an annual sum, the *don gratuit*, to the State. The topography of Paris and most other cities and towns was determined, not by office or insurance blocks, but by the domes and spires of churches and chapels. In the countryside the local church served as the focal point for the electoral, administrative and spiritual life of the community. The tolling of its bell dictated the rhythm of daily work as well as substituting for the modern fire alarm and police siren. The local seigneur had only one rival, the curé.

Yet, despite its universal influence, the Church in the eighteenth century was increasingly plagued by bitter criticism from its enemies and by dissension within its own ranks. The Philosophes learned to sharpen their wits on priests and monks. 'To learn the true principles of morality', wrote baron d'Holbach, 'men have no need of theology, of revelation, or gods: They have need only of reason.' Not all the Philosophes were as radical in their approach as d'Holbach, but they were fairly united in seeking to replace revelation by reason, in castigating the intolerance, the superstition, the barbarism of 'priestly religion'. Even Rousseau agreed that original thought was of greater value to man than the concept of original sin. Nor were criticisms of the Church confined to the relative few who could afford copies of the Encyclopedia, a work of vast erudition, rationalist in approach, which attracted contributions from leading authorities in the world of science and the arts. In urban, and indeed in parts of rural France, the lower orders were also becoming increasingly alienated from the Church. Anti-clericalism was spreading unevenly long before the Revolution as the scabrous literature disseminated by travelling book-sellers suggests. In the countryside the peasantry were all too often left to the mercy of priests whose instruction and education were at best rudimentary. The changing climate of opinion was best exemplified by the toleration afforded to Protestants, and to a lesser extent, to Jews. The former, representing no more than five per cent of the total population, were granted an Edict of Toleration by the State in 1787.

Although the learned assault of an articulate minority undoubtedly distorted the truth, many of the criticisms were justified. The Church certainly appeared at times to be more interested in protecting its privilege and wealth than furthering the spiritual well-being of its adherents. The Church paid less than five per cent of its revenue in taxes; half of the revenues of the great abbeys went to line the pockets of 'abbots' whose only real qualifications were their noble birth and the influence they exerted at Court. The archbishopric of Strasbourg was worth 400,000 livres a year; that of Paris over half a million. Many bishops, once secure in their sees, conveniently forgot to appear from one Easter communion to the next. The *dime*, a tax levied by the Church on the produce of the soil, brought in over 100 million livres a year. There was no uniformity in its collection—as little as one-fiftieth of the crop in parts of Dauphiné; as much as a quarter in parts of Brittany. The average percentage has been estimated at around one-fifteenth. In addition the Church was the single greatest landowning corporation in France. In the Nord, Picardy and the Brie region the Church might own up to one-third of the land, although in the Auvergne it was as little as three per cent. The regular clergy owned about a fifth of Paris and even in the South-East, where the Church was not a great land-owner, towns like Nîmes and Montpellier were dotted with church property. The wealth of the Church offered a tempting prize to the rational and impecunious revolutionary régimes.

The situation of the monastic orders was far more precarious. They had been declining in numbers and prestige (particularly the male and contemplative orders) throughout the century: in 1789 there were only 1,700 religious houses in France, about half the number which had existed in 1750. Louis XV had already expelled the Jesuits and seized some monastic property. Those orders responsible for running schools and hospitals still performed an invaluable service to the community; others had lost their *raison d'être*. In many areas freemasonry was being built on the ruins of monasticism. There were 700 lodges with over 30,000 members in France at the end of the century and it was by no means unknown for clerics and monks to take an active interest in the new faith which was more democratic and certainly more in keeping with the spirit of the age than monasticism. Jansenism, often described as 'the methodism of the Catholic Church' and the source of so much religious and political controversy in France since the reign of Louis XIV, had lost much of its vitality although it was still capable of precipitating the most unholy personal rows. There was also a marked absence of Christian charity in the relationship between the regular and the secular orders.

Perhaps the fundamental weakness of the Church, however, was the wide gulf which separated the higher from the lower clergy. Throughout the century the most important positions in the Church had gone to the aristocracy. Mercier, a perceptive if prejudiced contemporary observer, wrote in the 1780s, 'To whom do they give the bishoprics? To the nobles. The great abbeys? To the nobles. All the richest livings? To the nobility.' The 60,000 *curés* and *vicaires,* who conducted the daily routine of religious life, were obliged to live on a far more modest scale. One can find the occasional curé living quite comfortably: the incumbent of the parish of Saint Eustache in Paris could count on an income of 10,000 livres a year. But for every one of these there were hundreds living on a minimum wage of 750 livres (*vicaires* earned far less) which hardly raised them, in economic terms, above the poorest members of the peasantry they served. The resentment of the lower clergy gave birth to such movements as Richerism, which outlined a more democratic form of church government; it also provoked, during the critical debates leading to the formation of a National Assembly in the summer of 1789, their defection from the First Estate.

It was widely accepted, therefore, even within the Church, that

10 *The rapid depreciation of the assignats meant ruin for thousands of investors, hence the symbolic beggarly figure*

fundamental changes were necessary, although even in August 1789, when the Church lost its right to levy the *dîme* and the principle of religious toleration was established, few foresaw that the Revolution would launch its own crusade against religion. The key issue at the beginning of the Revolution was the expropriation of church property. Many deputies were a little apprehensive that this move might be interpreted as an attack upon the sanctity of private property. Objections on this score were overcome by announcing that the property of the Church could not be regarded as private; it belonged by right to the nation. The first 400 million livres of church lands were placed on the open market in December 1789. In less than three years about half had been sold. In order to expedite matters, and to secure desperately-needed funds, state creditors were paid off in paper-money called assignats with which they could purchase church lands. The assignats were then to be destroyed. It was an ingenious, simple, but disastrous scheme. The need for ready cash induced the Government to issue the assignats as ordinary currency; lack of confidence and forgery on a massive scale completed the process until by 1795 one needed a sackful of assignats to buy a cauliflower, let alone a church.

The sale of church lands, from which, due to the rapid depreciation of the assignats, the State gained comparatively little, did not provoke a major social upheaval. There was a vast transfer of ownership from the Church to private individuals, but these individuals usually came from the ranks of the bourgeoisie or the richer peasantry. Some land was sold in small lots but the general practice was to sell by auction which clearly benefited the more affluent. The bourgeoisie had been busily rounding-off their estates long before the Revolution; the sale of church lands accelerated the process. It did, however, associate hundreds of thousands of buyers with the revolutionary settlement, a fact of political rather than social significance.

The end of the Church as an independent order within the State, the abolition of the tithe, the sale of its lands, the attack on the monastic orders in February 1790, represent the more negative features of the religious settlement. In July, the deputies presented what they regarded as the more positive aspect with the publication of the Civil Constitution of the Clergy. It was a document which not only reflected the rational approach of the deputies, but also represented the culmination of a long Gallican tradition, a tradition, beginning with the Concordat of Francis I in 1516, which insisted on the rights of the French Crown and the clergy against the pretensions of Rome. The majority of the clergy were prepared to discuss, if not accept, its implications. It was the lack of adequate consultation, both with the clergy and the Papacy, which helped to provoke such bitter opposition.

The Constitution abolished the old diocesan organisation and replaced it with the much neater plan of one bishop for each of the eighty-three departments into which France had been divided. Bishops and curés were to be elected by the same voters who sent deputies to the Assembly: thus Protestants, and even atheists, could determine the choice of a Catholic prelate. The salaries of the lower clergy were substantially increased; the power of the Papacy seriously curtailed. The response of the clergy depended in the final analysis on the attitude of the Pope who, for various reasons, not all of them spiritual, took nearly eight months to pronounce his verdict. At the end of 1790, irritated by the dilatory tactics pursued at Rome, the deputies decided to expedite matters by demanding an oath of allegiance to the new Constitution. Only seven bishops and about half the lower clergy agreed to take the required oath, many of them with important qualifications. In parts of Western and North-Eastern France there were massive refusals. On 13 April 1791, the Pope confirmed the growing schism within the Church by denouncing the Constitution outright. Henceforth the French clergy were to be divided between those who had accepted the settlement, the constitutional clergy, and those who had rejected it, the refractory priests.

The unhappy and unforeseen consequences of these religious debates gave a tremendous boost to the forces of counter-revolution in France. Long-standing social and economic grievances were now aggravated by religious dissension; the rift between town and country grew noticeably wider. For the confused peasant the city-dweller was not only threatening his property but his God. In areas where Protestants and Catholics lived in close proximity religious differences led to open warfare. In the city of Nîmes, divided between a Catholic majority and an economically-dominant Protestant minority, violence erupted on a scale which was unprecedented since the religious wars of the sixteenth and early eighteenth centuries. Political agitators like François Froment fanned the flames of religious hatred by announcing that, 'ever since their arrival in France the Protestants have excited trouble, revolt, civil war and bloodshed'. In the summer of 1790, over 300 Catholics were massacred by Protestant National Guards encouraged, in the time-honoured tradition, by their peasant co-religionaries from the surrounding hills. In the West, where the great Vendean revolt was soon to break out, rumblings of the approaching storm could be heard long before 1793. Of the wounds inflicted or reopened by the Revolution none probed more deeply than those caused by religious differences.

Until the outbreak of war the Assembly was reluctant to treat the refractory clergy too harshly with the result that for over a year many villagers had the dubious advantage of being served by two priests in the same parish. The tensions which this spiritual duality produced even within a single household can easily be imagined. 1792 proved to be the real year of decision. In April, the Assembly declared war on the Austrian Emperor; a month later the first punitive measures were taken against refractory priests; on 10 August, the Tuileries were stormed by the Parisian crowd, the Monarchy overthrown and the first French Republic proclaimed. Not for a long time had the average Frenchman been confronted with so many difficult choices—for or against the local seigneur; for or against the Monarchy; war or peace; constitutional or refractory priest. As the military situation deteriorated with the allied armies advancing on Paris, opinions polarised more rapidly. Only a week after the downfall of the Monarchy more stringent laws, including the threat of deportation, were passed against refractory priests.

But whether one supported the refractory or constitutional priest the Revolution had completely altered the relationship between the Church and the individual. In September 1792, divorce was legalised and the registers of births, deaths and marriages taken out of the hands of the curé and handed over to the local municipalities, thus snapping

11 *Civil marriage became possible after the law of 20 September 1792*

one of the most important bonds which linked the individual to the Church. Later onslaughts on the meaning and purpose of the holy sacraments were to place severe strain on the more spiritual ties. The constitutional priest, elected like the local mayor, deprived of many electoral and administrative functions, was but a pale shadow of the *ancien régime* curé. What of the village school where the curé had taught thousands of peasant children the catechism and at least the rudiments of literacy? For the most deprived sections of the community, what alternative was provided for the almshouses and charitable foundations which, in times of acute misery, had at least alleviated their suffering? For the devotees of Voltaire and Diderot the modernisation of the Church meant coming to terms with reality and reason: for the poor, the beggars, the maimed and the blind it meant increased hardship.

During the next two years, as Catholicism became increasingly identified in the popular mind with counter-revolution, refractory, even constitutional priests, were to be subjected to a relatively short but severe spasm of persecution. In Bordeaux on 14 July 1792, during celebrations to commemorate the fall of the Bastille, a refractory priest was decapitated by an enraged crowd, his head impaled on the end of a pole and carried around the streets to shouts of 'Vive la Constitution! Mort aux prêtres! A bas les refractaires!'

As for those priests crowded into the prisons of the capital, their fate became more problematic with every league covered by the advancing foreign armies. Some had undoubtedly plotted against the régime; the majority were simply caught up in the inexorable logic of a revolution-ary and wartime crisis which so readily makes 'traitors' of the uncom-mitted. The massacre of a group of priests being transferred from the Abbaye prison on 2 September provided the signal for the most savage outburst of popular fury during the entire course of the Revolution. In two bloody days, three bishops and over 200 priests were brutally murdered. The educated wife of a deputy in the Assembly wrote: 'Atrocious necessity . . . heads cut off, priests massacred. I cannot bring myself to give you the details although my reason tells me that the Prussians . . . would have done as much and worse. My God! Pity the people who are provoked into acts of such terrible carnage.' Unfortun-ately the September massacres marked only the beginning of a long calvary for the clergy. In just over a year, thousands joined the ranks of the émigrés, many in England where a Protestant monarch placed his estates in Winchester at their disposal.

So far, however, the religious attitudes of the people had been challenged rather than revolutionised. It was during the Terror that the most conscious and the most determined effort was made to eradicate 'several centuries of prejudice and ignorance'. Possibly the most revolutionary act was the introduction of a new calendar in October 1793. Intended, like Hitler's Reich, to last a thousand years, it was all but forgotten in less than a decade. Dating from 22 September 1792 (the date when the First Republic had been proclaimed), it was divided into twelve months, each of thirty days with five 'supplementary days' added to make the requisite number of 365. The months were given new names—Vendémiaire, Floréal, Messidor, etc., and the week was abolished in favour of the *décade* lasting ten days. Hence 22 September became, in accordance with the new Calendar, 1 Vendémiaire Year I.

In an attempt to create the new revolutionary man, the rhythm of everyday life, hitherto determined by feast days and the Sabbath, was totally disrupted. The departmental council of the Indre-et-Loire announced in November 1793 that 'the term Sunday is abolished. It is an offence therefore for workers, manufacturers, street sellers . . . to work, shop or trade on such days'. The penalty for transgressing this law was an appearance before the Revolutionary Tribunal. In practice, however, it proved difficult to disrupt traditional patterns of social behaviour. Although employers may have welcomed the nine-day working week, the workers were understandably less enthusiastic. The custom of meeting and drinking in the favoured *cabarets* on the outskirts of the cities on Sunday, often extended to Monday (a notable day of absenteeism under the *ancien régime*), was not easily broken.

Even before the Revolutionary Calendar had been introduced anti-clerical, and indeed anti-religious, sentiment had been gathering momentum. In Paris and the provinces, municipalities were busily changing places and street-names to reflect more accurately the republican dawn. The place Louis-le-Grand in Paris was altered to place des piques; the section Croix-rouge became the bonnet rouge; St Tropez was converted into Héraclée. Doting republican parents conferred noble Roman names like Cato and Brutus upon their offspring: citizen Lebrun thought that Civilization-Jemappes-République

12 *A dechristianisation ceremony in a provincial town*

might suit his infant daughter! On 27 September 1793, the Convention announced a new series of feast-days beginning with the *fête de l'agriculture* and ending in August with a celebration of old age.

This 'dechristianisation' movement reached its peak in the autumn and winter of 1793-4 with the dispatch of *représentants en mission* to the provinces. Fouché in the Nièvre department set the tone by demanding that all priests, whether they had sworn allegiance to the Constitution or not, should abjure their shameful professions and fill their lives with the worship of Reason. 'Death', Fouché announced to an unbelieving multitude, 'was an eternal sleep'. Supported by a motley gathering of foreigners, 'intellectuals' and demagogues, like the journalist Hébert, the movement gained momentum with the closing of churches, the destruction of relics and statues and the seizure of church plate, silver and bells for the war effort. The campaign was not sponsored by the Jacobin-controlled Committee of Public Safety, although certain members were sympathetic; more often than not it occurred spontaneously, arising in the towns, but also in some rural areas, from a long history of anti-clericalism. On occasions, the less enthusiastic

members of a local Popular Society were prodded into action by a visit
from a battalion of regular troops on its way to the front or by the
arrival of a detachment of the 'Revolutionary Army'—volunteer
organisations recruited in Paris and the major provincial cities and
towns to ensure a continuing flow of food-supplies and to 'politicise'
the surrounding countryside.

Frequently the dechristianisers compounded anti-feminism with
anti-clericalism. In the department of the Gers, the Representative-on-
Mission, doubtless to the surprise of the local housewives, informed
the latter that they were 'all prostitutes of the priests, especially those
of you who attend their *foutues* masses and take part in their buffoonery'.
In some areas the dechristianisers were not slow to indulge in buffoonery
of their own design. In Boulogne-sur-mer, during the course of
an anti-clerical procession, the Pope was depicted as a magpie and a
Vendean priest as a hypocrite with one hand on his heart, the other

13   *An anti-Jacobin print illustrating the Feast of Reason held in
Notre-Dame in November 1793*

14 *A Vendean rebel asks the Virgin Mary to bless his struggle against the godless Republic*

hiding a dagger—a faithful reproduction of the identification of the clergy with the counter-revolution. In Paris, the Archbishop himself was prevailed upon to resign his functions and, so that there should be no mistaking his motivation, replace his mitre with the red Cap of Liberty. The climax of the campaign in the capital came on 10 November when Notre-Dame resounded, not to the Catholic liturgy or the singing of the psalms, but to the exhortations of the 'Goddess of Reason'.

In the West and the South-East, where the cause of the counter-revolution had attracted most support, priests were regarded—often quite rightly—as the main obstacle to the indoctrination of the revolutionary gospel. At Nantes, boats filled with priests were floated on to the fast-moving river Loire then deliberately sunk taking their human cargo down with them. Well over a hundred priests and nuns met their death in Lyons, victims of the mass executions ordered by Representatives Fouché and Collot d'Herbois. Hundreds more were left to rot in prisons or, as in the port of Rochefort, in old slaving ships hastily converted into floating dungeons.

Dechristianisation, unleashed by the civil and military authorities, evoked a sympathetic response in the hearts of the *petit peuple*: anticlericalism had a long and honoured tradition in France. But if Catholicism could be abandoned, at least temporarily, the break was too sudden to smother every kind of religious manifestation. In many instances the rhetoric of Catholicism was translated to serve the worship of the infant Republic. Women lit candles before statues of Marat, one of the most radical and sanguinary of the republican heroes who had been assassinated in the summer of 1793, chanting, 'O sacred heart of Marat'; a housewife noted in her diary that the Revolution had provided such overwhelming proof of the treachery of the aristocracy that 'even the blind see, the lame walk and the friends of humanity bless Heaven'. The Revolution had its own saints—Chalier, Marat, Lepeletier, the latter's body being displayed in public complete with wounds and bloody linen. The worship of Marat grew into a real cult. In a sense this idolatry was more meaningful to the popular classes than the rational Deism of the bourgeoisie: if the English had Methodism as an emotional safety-valve, the French had *maratism*.

The new anti-faith did not, however, satisfy the aspirations of Rousseauist admirers like Robespierre; besides, although dechristianisation was in many ways a transitory phenomenon, it did provoke massive resistance from certain sections of the peasantry. In the Seine-et-Marne department peasants from the villages around Rozoy invaded the town on 13 December 1793 shouting 'Vive la religion catholique! . . . we want the mass, Sundays and feast-days'. The severity of Carrier and Fouché's repressive missions in Nantes and Lyons and the iconoclastic activities of detachments of the Parisian Revolutionary Army around Auxerre began to alarm a government which, in the midst of a war-time crisis, sought unity above all else. Hence, for political as much as religious reasons, the Committee of Public Safety decided to recall its Representatives and to denounce dechristianisers like Hébert as 'agents of the aristocracy'. To fill the void left by the collapse of the Catholic and Protestant cults, Robespierre and his colleagues decided to introduce the worship of the Supreme Being, a concept closely related to the intellectual deism of the eighteenth century. On 8 June 1794, Robespierre himself led a vast procession to inaugurate the new faith. In the garden of the Tuileries an effigy of Atheism was set alight to reveal from within its depths a rather sooty statue of Wisdom. A few weeks later Robespierre and his colleagues had been arrested and guillotined: the cult of the Supreme Being died with them.

15   *A Catholic priest celebrating a clandestine marriage-ceremony during the Terror*

For those Frenchmen with at least the faint stirrings of religious sentiment, but prepared nonetheless to follow the lead of the various revolutionary régimes (people had not yet adjusted to the idea of religion being separate from government), the sequence of events must have been extraordinarily confusing—Catholic in 1789, Constitutional in 1791, dechristianised in 1793 and finally 'Rousseauised' in 1794. For the next few years, with religions exploding on all sides, the French were left to pick their own way delicately through the minefield. Some municipalities continued to pursue anti-clerical policies: in the South-East the most anti-clerical Representatives arrived after the fall of the Robespierrists. One could still find the odd Temple of Reason, but on the whole with the attempted reconstruction of the Constitutional Church under its leader Grégoire and the return, or re-emergence from hiding, of many refractory priests there was a groundswell of opinion moving from below in favour of a return to some form of religious faith. This was recognised by the Thermidorean regime when, on 21 February 1795, a bill was passed legalising public worship, but within strictly defined limits. The State refused to contribute financially to any cult; all outward signs of worship, such as bells or processions, were expressly forbidden; in short the Church, for the first time in its history, was disestablished. The Government still expressed the rather forlorn hope that, given time and the right education, the people would come to appreciate the superior virtues of Reason over Religion.

If many regions, like the departments in the centre of France still bore the imprint of dechristianisation, elsewhere the faithful began to flock back to the churches. Bishop Grégoire hastened to give the Constitutional Church some administrative unity and to attract other bishops and priests back to their sees and parishes. The degree of enthusiasm exhibited suggests that religion was still alive, if not exactly kicking: the Bishop of Amiens regretted that, although church attendance was reasonably good, 'few bother to observe feast-days whilst plays and other public amusements are patronised everywhere'. The fact was that the Constitutional Church had lost its *raison d'être*. As Professor McManners notes, on the eve of Napoleon's seizure of power it 'stood revealed as an historical accident, neither the Church of of a nation nor the Church of a reformation'.

As for those Catholics who had refused to compromise their principles by joining the Constitutional Church their situation was far more precarious, particularly after the elections of 1797 which, revealing as they did a resurgence of royalist opinion in the country, provoked a discredited and nervous government into one final bout of persecution. Priests were deported to penal colonies or left to rot in old slaving ships. Although less dramatic than under the Terror the persecution of the period 1797-1799 was far more costly in terms of human suffering. Since most of the refractory clergy who escaped arrest were either in exile or had left the priesthood, religious life for the 'orthodox' Catholics had to be organised secretly by private individuals. Predictably, persecution served only to increase the fervour of the faithful. As the daughter of a former seigneur noted in her memoirs: 'The dangers inherent in our forbidden service added to the solemnity of the occasion. Kneeling silently on the floor our prayers rose on wings of fire . . . those nightly and secret reunions recalled the persecution of the early christians.' One of the difficulties facing orthodox Catholics, however, was the capture of Rome by the French troops and the imprisonment of the Pope who died in captivity in August 1799.

It is, perhaps, peculiarly fitting that, in France at least, the ninety-ninth year of the eighteenth century should have been one of almost total exhaustion. Political intrigue and corruption in government circles; apathy, and in places, anarchy amongst the people; religious life disrupted and discredited. The literate and governing élite did attempt to inject a little moral purpose into the revolutionary corpse by the introduction of yet another cult—Theophilanthropy. An austere creed, Theophilanthropy was dedicated to the worship of nature and morality. The faithful—and there were never very many—were subjected to long sermons on married love, the marvels of nature and the duties of man in society. This, the last revolutionary curtsey to eighteenth-century deism, was only a little more successful than Robespierre's earlier version, the cult of the Supreme Being.

The bells which chimed in the new century also heralded a renewed interest in religion. Scepticism and deism were beginning to lose their

16   *A devotee of the cult of Theophilanthropy. The pyramid is a manifestation of God's will in History*

attraction for the richer bourgeoisie and indeed not a few intellectuals appeared to have had a surfeit of Supreme Beings. Religion was regarded as not only indispensable for keeping the masses in line (the bourgeoisie had always believed this, although events during the Revolution had hardened their conviction), but also as the fashionable thing to have. Madame Delarue, the wife of a rich banker, took the collection at the church of Saint-Roch 'preceded by a Russian count and followed by a negro and two lacqueys carrying her train'. The great success of Chateaubriand's *Génie du christianisme*—a lyrical poem on the attractions of the Catholic ceremonial—can only be explained by the influence of Romanticism which drew so heavily on religious themes. In the beginning, as at the end of the nineteenth century, it was aesthetism not ascetism which attracted the faithful back to the altar. Certain intellectual fraternities like the *Institut* might anticipate Nietzsche by declaring that God was dead, the Army might remain true to its anticlerical heritage, but for someone as pragmatic and authoritarian as Napoleon Bonaparte the facts were reasonably straightforward: religion—Fouché and the *Institut* notwithstanding—was not dead; the counter-revolution, which had recruited so many of its adherents on a religious ticket, continued to pose a threat to the integrity of the State; Catholic countries like Belgium, which had been overrun by French armies, might well accommodate themselves more willingly to their new masters if the latter were to divest themselves of their godless clothing. Napoleon was also not slow to appreciate the benefits which might accrue, in terms of prestige and propaganda, from a reconciliation with the Church.

The election of a more pliable Pope, Pius VII, made it easier for the two parties to reach agreement, and although the famous Concordat of 1801 was to take a year to negotiate, it was to govern Church-State relationships in France for over a century. The Concordat, buttressed by the important Organic Articles, was Gallican in inspiration: effective control of the Church in France was to be left in the hands of the Government. The State appointed the bishops who then chose the lower clergy; all salaries were to be paid by the State. The document recognized the alienation of church property since 1789 (indispensable if the bourgeoisie were to support the agreement) and the Catholic faith was not, as the Papacy desired, to become the sole religion of the

17   *Pius VII hands a copy of the Concordat to Cardinal Consalvi,*
responsible for the negotiations with Napoleon

State but 'the religion of the greater majority of Frenchmen', the
clumsy phraseology reflecting the degree of disunity which still per-
sisted in France. De Maistre, the outstanding—if somewhat un-
balanced—theoretician of the extreme Right was moved to express the
opinion that, 'The crimes of an Alexander Borgia are less revolting
than this hideous apostasy by his weak-kneed successor'.

Nevertheless the Pope had brought the eldest daughter of the Church
back to Rome; provision was made for the return of a few of the
religious orders. Catholicism had emerged from the Revolution bloody
but unbowed. The Protestant Church was reorganised at the same
time, giving unprecedented power to the pastor and overall control
of the Church to the bourgeoisie. The Protestant clergy were, like their
Catholic colleagues, to be financed by the Government. The Jewish
community was obliged to wait a few more years before they were
grouped into territorial units controlled by the Sanhedrin, although the
Government favoured a long-term policy of assimilation.

There was some initial difficulty over the appointment of bishops for
the re-established Church, but eventually an amalgam of refractory
and constitutional clergy was agreed upon. A minority of *ancien
régime* bishops refused to apply for vacant sees and formed their own
schism—*la petite église*—unrecognised both by Napoleon and the

Pope. The problem of launching the Concordat was to prove far less intractable than that of keeping the settlement afloat, particularly as Napoleon's expanding imperial vision collided with the Pope's interests as a secular ruler. Nevertheless there were many reasons why, at least in the early years of the Empire, Catholics should have looked so benevolently upon their new ruler, one of the most important being the influence they were allowed to exercise in the field of education.

Under the *ancien régime*, the great majority of children who had received any education could thank either the curé or the teaching orders like the Brothers of the Christian Life which had over one thousand members on the eve of the Revolution. The Brothers had laid great emphasis on the importance of recruiting children at an early age before, as the abbé Barbotin phrased it, they were corrupted 'by lustful passions'. The Revolution had attempted to eradicate what it increasingly regarded as the pernicious influence of the Church in education, preferring to inculcate in the young the 'natural' precepts of Rousseau as enunciated in his didactic novel *Emile*. Many progressive and ingenious schemes were drawn up, but the deputies failed to find either the time or the money to implement them. During the Terror, the sans-culottes had constantly implored the authorities to educate them to the responsibilities of living in the new Jerusalem, agreeing with a

18   *An idealised image of the Republican mother instructing her child in the Rights of Man*

schoolmaster in the rue de Sévres that a study of the Constitution 'should be the primary object of their instruction'.

In 1795, the Revolution had actually produced a new scheme of education. Alongside the creation or reconstitution of such notable institutions as the *Ecole Polytechnique* or the *Conservatoire des Arts et Métiers*, a network of secondary schools—the *écoles centrales*—had been introduced. These schools had been based on the royal *collèges* and retained a very strong emphasis on classical studies. Although, by 1799, many departments could boast of at least one school the scheme had never been an unqualified success. The majority of parents continued to send their children to private establishments, either because of the distances involved or because they distrusted these new and as yet unproven institutions. Their real significance lies in the fact that they, and the old royal colleges, provided the blueprints for Napoleon's far more successful experiment—the lycées.

It was in 1802 that the famous lycées—state secondary schools—were created, their curriculum based on classical languages, rhetoric and logic, at the expense of modern languages and history. They were designed principally to produce the military and administrative cadres essential to the smooth running of Napoleon's Empire. Partly for this reason, the schools were run on para-military lines complete with drums and uniforms for the recruits. The lycées, destined to become the backbone of the French educational system, were slow to develop—there were only thirty-seven operating in 1808—partly because money was lacking but also because of stiff competition from the private sector.

This competition induced Napoleon to tighten his control over education: in 1808 the Imperial University was founded. Members of the University were given a virtual monopoly of teaching at the primary, secondary and higher levels, although again lack of adequate funds prevented Napoleon from abolishing all private establishments. Clerical influence was by no means eliminated; indeed, under the Grand-Master of the University, Fontanes, the influence of the Church was increased by giving the clergy considerable powers of inspection and supervision. The State hardly bothered with primary education: according to one contemporary writer primary schools were only designed to offer the lower orders the rudiments of literacy so that 'they could more readily devote themselves to domestic or agricultural labour, or enter workshops'. This concept of the dual role of education— one for the masses and one for the élite—has bedevilled French education almost to the present day.

In religious life, as in education, France under Napoleon was centralised and bureaucratised. Napoleon rarely conceived of an institution without wondering what purpose it would serve in the glorification of himself and his Empire. The clergy were obliged to use their considerable influence on behalf of the State: the pulpit, in an age of illiteracy, was the main avenue of communication between government and people. New variations were added to the traditional themes of the virtues of poverty and obedience—patriotism and the deification of Napoleon. Congregations were treated to extracts taken from the Bulletins of the Grande Armée, and informed that the paths of conscription, as much as those of holiness, led to Heaven. The Bishop of Aix reminded his parishioners that Napoleon, 'like a latter-day Moses, was called from the deserts of Egypt'. Police spies often mingled with worshippers on Sundays: as Fouché, the Minister of Police, noted somewhat cynically, 'There is more than one similarity between their (the priests') functions and mine'.

In return for the invaluable assistance of the Church, Napoleon ensured that religion was placed on a more secure footing than at any time since the beginning of the Revolution. By 1810 communes had been charged with the responsibility of maintaining religious buildings and of subsidising the salaries of the clergy; the State itself contributed almost fifty million francs a year in additional salaries and pensions. There were over 2,000 female religious establishments in France by the end of the Empire whilst the Brothers of the Christian Schools and the Lazarists were reasserting much of their former influence over education, particularly at the primary level. Clearly, a great deal remained to be done so far as recruitment to the clergy and the re-building of church premises were concerned, but Napoleon's contribution to the restoration of both Catholicism and Protestantism in France cannot easily be dismissed.

The break with the Papacy in 1808, however, precipitated not only by Napoleon's economic and military policies but also by his jealousy of the spiritual authority of the Pope, provoked visible signs of discontent among many Catholics. As Georges Léfebvre has noted: 'The Concordat had deprived royalist and counter-revolutionary movements of the support of the clergy; the break with the Pope restored it to them'. Catholic organisations like¯ the *Congrégation*, founded by Father Delpuis, and the *Chevaliers de la Foi* began to recruit an increasing number of adherents, providing a focal point for opposition to the Emperor and preparing the way for a return to a truly Catholic and royalist régime. The village priest was alienated from Napoleon by the protracted and bitter struggle with the Pope and the Council of Bishops over the vexed issue of canonical institution. The attempt to integrate the Catholic Church into the French Imperium, involving as it did the imprisonment of the Pope, proved to be a dismal failure, the most utopian of Napoleon's grandiose schemes.

The return of the Bourbons, their policies influenced by extremist opinion among the émigrés, created a more suitable, if largely artificial climate for religious life. Catholicism was reinstated as the religion of the State, which provoked much panic and alarm amongst the Protestant community; education was placed more firmly than ever in the hands of the clergy; observance of the Sabbath was made compulsory. Despite this outward manifestation of the Church's power, however, it proved impossible to return to the 'good old days' of the *ancien régime*. The Church had lost its landed property and the right to levy the tithe; it no longer existed as a separate order within the State; it was forced to compete with the State in the field of education. What is perhaps more important, anti-clericalism had bitten more deeply into the French psyche. When Napoleon returned from the island prison of Elba in 1815 he was greeted in Paris with cries of 'Long live the Emperor! Down with the priests'. The Revolution had politicised anti-clericalism. It was to remain one of the most divisive factors in French society and politics throughout the nineteenth century.

3   The Transformation of Peasant Society

The changes described in the preceding two chapters affected the peasantry (over three-quarters of the total population of France) to a greater degree than any other section of the community. It was far easier for the city or town-dweller to escape the influence of the seigneur and the curé. The Revolution destroyed the fabric of village society, undermining the power and prestige of the nobility, questioning the basic assumptions of religious life, sharpening antagonisms within the peasant community itself. As a result of the Revolution vast amounts of property were thrown onto the open market, whetting the already keen appetite of the peasant for land. After a generation of war hundreds of thousands of peasants were never to return to their native fields. Perhaps it was the time and energy devoted to these momentous problems which helps to explain why, in the same period, no great change occurred in the cultivation of the soil.

The peasantry owned about one-third of the land, concentrated, as one might expect, mainly in the poorer and more remote regions. In Flanders, Picardy or the great granaries of the Beauce and the Brie around the capital, peasant property was not extensive. It was in the North-West that Arthur Young noted during his travels through France that 'the richest scenes of cultivation are to be found'. It was in these same regions that the percentage of landless peasants might rise to over seventy per cent. In much poorer areas like the Limousin peasant properties might account for over half the land cultivated. It was here that Young was reminded 'of the misery of Ireland . . . the country girls and women do without shoes or stockings'. Most French peasants were not serfs, tied to the soil and their masters: less than one million fell into this category. The great majority regarded themselves as free men, owning and disposing of their property within traditionally-defined limits. If they owned property on a noble estate, and there were relatively few who did not, the peasants paid the *cens* or *champart*, occasionally both, in recognition of the seigneur's

19 *Recruits to the reserve army of the* ancien régime *the* milice, *were chosen by lot. Here the peasant is asking providence to protect him from the privilege of serving*

sovereignty, for 'the seigneurie represented the corner-stone of the social edifice of France'. In addition to the multiplicity of feudal dues and services outlined in a previous chapter the peasant was also obliged to pay the tithe to the Church and the *taille* to the government, the latter tax being a particularly heavy load on his already over-burdened shoulders.

The paradox of regarding themselves as property-owners, and yet paying dues to a lord in order to dispose of their property as they wished, had occasioned only sporadic protests among the peasantry until, in the second half of the eighteenth century, the seigneurs and the bourgeoisie began to exploit their estates more efficiently. Frequently the nobility leased their property to merchants, lawyers or even the wealthier farmers, often endowed with a more developed sense of business acumen. The property was then sublet to share-croppers or small farmers usually on short leases of four to nine years duration. The existence of a growing number of wealthy peasants, the *laboureurs*,

20   *A rural scene of the Midi of France*

who provided grain for the markets, work for the landless and mortgage facilities for the improverished, was provoking serious conflicts within the peasant community before 1789.

Such peasants, owning perhaps the only plough in the village, and acting as amateur lawyers and administrators, were far more in touch with urban life and in a good position to exploit the sale of church lands after 1789. The rich tenant-farmer who rented big tracts of land in the better agricultural regions of northern France, Normandy, the Brie and the Beauce also benefited. The vast majority of peasants, however, fell into neither of these categories, consisting of small-owners (*petits propriétaires*), share-croppers (*métayers*) and day-labourers (*journaliers*). By 1826, over seventy per cent of French peasants were farming less than twelve acres.

The share-cropping system was the most common form of agricultural labour in France, particularly in parts of the West, the Centre and the South-West. The share-cropper received the seed and occasionally the necessary farm implements in return for up to a half of the produce at harvest time. It was a miserable system, perpetuating poverty and ignorance, but it did at least provide hundreds of thousands of peasants with some sort of stake in the soil. It also raised them above the level of the day-labourer, who was often thrown out of work once the harvest had been gathered in, and left to swell the ranks of the beggars and brigands who plagued the French countryside before and during the revolutionary period.

The above résumé provides a very over-simplified picture of rural life; it reduces the complex system of landholding to its simplest terms; it takes no account of the thousands of village artisans like blacksmiths, carpenters, wheelwrights or of the violent and usually ostracised groups of wood-cutters, charcoal-burners, clog-makers, who moved from region to region, often living like animals in forest huts, and frequently crossing the narrow frontier between respectability and rural crime.

One should also emphasise the importance of domestic industry in the French countryside. In Normandy, Alsace, Languedoc, wherever textile industries were based, the peasant usually supplemented his meagre income by finishing-off silk, cloth or woollen goods for a merchant-manufacturer. Arthur Young, travelling from Rouen to Le Havre, found 'farm-houses and cottages everywhere and the cotton manufacture in all'. In Languedoc, the great majority of peasants, particularly in the Protestant districts, grew raw silk or had a loom upon which the whole family worked during the winter months. The size of domestic industry in France, and the existence of a huge reservoir of labour, helps to explain why the country did not industrialise at the same pace as Britain in the eighteenth century.

In a way it was the conservatism of the French peasantry which swelled the rising tide of discontent in the countryside on the eve of the Revolution. It was not that the vast majority of peasants were becoming poorer; indeed, since agricultural prices rose by sixty per cent in the course of the century, many were making increased profits from the sale of grain on the open market. It was the attack upon

21 *A popular lady in early nineteenth-century France: the seller of refreshing herbal drinks*

traditional customs and contracts which provoked the anger of the French peasant. More often than not peasants rioted to protect what they had, not to 'revolutionise' the system. The seizure of communal lands by the lords; the revision of old charters laying down the precise nature of feudal obligations; the increasing rapacity of the *laboureur* class; the law of June 1787 which destroyed what remained of the old democratic village assembly, handing over effective control to the notables—all this contributed to a growing sense of unease and dissatisfaction. The disastrous harvest of 1788, occurring as it did when the textile and wine industries were still suffering from a serious slump, exacerbated an already tense situation.

It was in these circumstances that the Government asked the peasants, in February 1789, to draw up lists of grievances which would be presented to the States-General at their meeting in the following May. These lists, or *cahiers de doléances*, reflect the misery and poverty of many small-owners, share-croppers and day-labourers as well as a more general hatred of the tithe, aspects of the feudal system and the inequality of taxation. The very act of meeting to discuss the preparation of the cahiers produced a new sense of purpose and hope. In May, the States-General duly met at Versailles, but as the weeks passed in what appeared to be endless constitutional wrangling, the peasantry began to take matters into their own hands.

During the spring of 1789 there had been many isolated reports of attacks on grain convoys and peasants congregating outside the farm-gates of a wealthy *laboureur* demanding grain at 'popular prices'. In July and August, provoked beyond measure by soaring bread prices and political events in Paris, peasant riots assumed a new and more violent form with the burning and plundering of chateaux and monasteries and the destruction of feudal records and contracts. Some of the worst scenes of violence were enacted in the North-East, although the repercussions of the movement were felt in many provinces. The forces of order were either too few or too sympathetic to contain the violence with the result that many noble familes were obliged to flee or to promise an end to the exaction of feudal payments and service. These widespread disturbances provided an admirable pretext for the settlement of personal feuds, the renunciation of long-standing debts and, particularly in Alsace which had a large Jewish population, a renewed outburst of anti-semitism. Some property-owners organised resistance in the larger towns and villages: at the famous monastery of Cluny in the Maconnais scores of peasants were shot or strung up on hastily-erected gallows as a grim warning of middle-class susceptibilities concerning attacks on property rights.

The eruption of violence, news of the fall of the Bastille in Paris, and the very real misery of many peasants in a period of acute economic shortage, all help to explain the escalation of agrarian revolt into the 'Great Fear' of 1789 (see pages 21–2). With the memory of one bad harvest behind them and the wheat ripening in the fields the peasantry tended to be singularly receptive to reports of aristocratic plots and the imminent arrival of 'the brigands'. A cloud of dust on the horizon made by a passing carriage, exaggerated reports transmitted from village to village by travellers, the sight of a stranger in a local inn, precipitated shock-waves of panic and alarm which spread in just over a fortnight from northern France to the Mediterranean. There were of course brigands roaming the countryside: a cahier from the province of Picardy referred to 'poor beggars, and strangers who were becoming brigands, thieves and fire-raisers', but the traditional rural trinity of rumour, plot and fear exaggerated the truth out of all proportion. The comte des Echerolles, who owned property in the Nivernais, tells us that in his locality, 'The terror was so widespread that we saw bands of peasants arriving from all parts armed with scythes and pitchforks determined to march against the brigands, but demanding to know where they could be found.' 'Les brigands' were not the less important in the spread of the Great Fear for being largely imaginary.

The famous decree passed on 'the night of 4 August' 1789, which purported to abolish feudalism in its entirety, was wrung from a reluctant Assembly, partly in response to the above events. Subsequent debates, as well as the definitive decrees published in the spring of 1790, indicated that the National Assembly was determined to defend, if not the right of privilege, then certainly the sanctity of property. All forms of 'personal' servitude were in fact abolished, along with the seigneurial courts, the tithe, provincial and municipal privileges. Seigneurial dues, however, were not abolished but, unless the peasant could prove that such dues had been exacted from him by force which, in the great majority of cases he could not, they were declared redeemable by purchase over twenty or twenty-five years. There is no doubt that a death-blow had been struck at the privileged nature of *ancien régime* society; there is equally no doubt that for the majority of peasants, convinced that the seigneurs had seized their lands by violence and usurpation in the irredeemable past, the solution proposed by the government was totally unsatisfactory. The logic of a revolutionary situation clashed with that of lawyers and property-owners.

Revolutionary logic triumphed. Open rebellion in a few areas, and passive resistance to the payment of any dues in many more, eventually obliged the deputies in Paris to revise their ingenious compromise. In August 1791, Arthur Young noted that 'associations amongst the peasantry . . . have been formed for the purpose of refusing to pay rents'. Sympathetic as he was to the peasant cause he felt constrained to comment that, 'in a country where such things are possible, property of every kind is in a dubious situation': precisely the problem which had vexed the Assembly since 1789! The outbreak of war leading indirectly to the advent of a Jacobin Government in 1793 finally resolved the crisis in favour of the peasantry. In the summer of 1793, anxious to gain national support for the war-effort, the Government conceded in fact what the peasants had gained in theory in 1789—the total abolition of feudal services and payments. Although unjust in its application to many land-owners it was to be of the greatest importance in associating the mass of the peasantry with the Revolution.

The peasantry was far less fortunate in satisfying its hunger for land, despite the vast tracts of Church and émigré property placed on the open market after 1789. The decree of 14 May 1790 did provide for the sale of such land in small lots and offered the peasant reasonable time to finance the operation. Peasant syndicates were formed to purchase big estates for later sub-division amongst their members, but six months later the government applied severe restrictions,

22   *The interior of a well-to-do peasant household in Brittany*

reducing the time allowed for payment and forbidding division of property into small lots. From 1793 to 1795, a certain amount of émigré property was put up for sale and it appears that in a few areas the peasantry did benefit. In certain regions of the Nord department the amount of land owned by the peasantry rose from thirty to forty per cent between 1789 and 1804. It has been estimated (although it should be stressed that such conclusions are rather tenuous) that the number of peasant small-owners increased by well over a million from 1789 to 1815, although the total amount of land cultivated by the peasantry did not substantially increase. It is true that many other factors, apart from the purchase of National Lands, were operating to produce a nation of peasant small-owners and that, compared with the gains made by the middle classes, the peasantry did not accomplish very much. Nonetheless, for the wealthier peasants at least, the early years of the Revolution had proved quite beneficial.

Only in one respect can it be said that the Revolution 'capitalised' the agricultural sector of the economy. This process involved the transformation of village life from a collective to an individualistic basis. Certain laws encouraged the division of communal lands in the village; others made it far easier for the peasant to grow what crops he pleased than to be restricted in his choice by custom. This freedom could only be exercised at the cost of the poorest small-owner and landless labourer; the loss of communal rights proved to be a severe blow for the most miserable section of the peasant community. It is also true that the transformation of village life occurred very slowly. As late as 1892 it was still necessary to introduce legislation giving the municipality the right to decide on the abandonment of collective grazing rights. Revolutionary legislation, however, like the influence of the Enclosure Act on an English village, did mark a decisive stage in the break-up of the village as a community.

Released from the burdens of feudalism, the peasantry, or rather that section of the peasantry which produced food and wine for the towns, was to be imprisoned by the controlled economy of the Terror. Although many made a fortune on the 'black market', the machinery of repression devised by the Committee of Public Safety brought government much closer to the peasants than at any time under the *ancien régime*. The Terror meant a detachment of the Revolutionary

Army, or a *commissaire des subsistances*, poking about in the barn for hoarded grain supplies, or possibly closing down the local church. The Government, faced with a critical wartime situation, did its best to requisition food for the armies and the towns but, lacking a modern bureaucracy, was only partially successful. Imprisoning or executing a farmer for hoarding was not the best way to ensure constant supplies of food and the resistance practised by many local authorities effectively frustrated all but the most energetic of the Government's Representatives-on-Mission.

Once the Government, by the decree of 29 September 1793, had fixed a ceiling, or General Maximum, on basic food supplies, the rich farmer, living on the expectation of higher prices, had the same interest as the poorest day-labourer in ensuring that grain did not leave his village. One of the major tasks of the Revolutionary Army was to break down resistance such as that encountered by the sergeant-major of the Compiègne detachment who reported that one peasant, when asked for wine had replied, 'that he had plenty, but it was not for sale at the price fixed by the Maximum . . . he didn't care a damn about the Maximum since those who had thought up the idea had only done so in order to get their hands on his property'.

The Terror undoubtedly sharpened antagonisms between the town and the countryside: the Revolutionary Army addressed placards to 'the inhabitants of the countryside' from 'their brothers in the towns', promising that unless the requisite supplies of grain were forthcoming the guillotine was only too anxious to perform its civic duties. The importance of bread supplies to the urban population is reflected in the following extract from a petition of the 48 Sections of Paris on 12 February 1793: 'The people must have bread, because without bread there is no law, no liberty and no Republic.' If the towns were not requisitioning grain (paid for by the assignat which the peasant, with every justification, detested) or imposing dechristianisation on the countryside, they were sending out merchants, lawyers or rentiers who were eagerly buying up property which the peasant coveted for himself. In the West, as Professor Tilly has shown, 'the bourgeois were the principal beneficiaries of the sales of church property'. The identification of the town-dweller with the purchase of National Lands and the propagation of anti-religious doctrines was one of the

23   *The arrest of a Breton royalist in 1793*

distinguishing features of the revolt of the peasantry against the
Republic in the Year II. In the South-East, as late as 1815, Protestant
merchants were being attacked as 'purchasers of National Lands at
the beginning of the Revolution'.

Some groups did benefit from the controlled economy introduced
under the Terror: rural consumers like day-labourers, village artisans,
and the army of black-marketeers or *revendeurs* waiting a mile or so
outside the towns in order to purchase grain from the villages which
was then sold, clandestinely, at prices above the Maximum. On the
whole, however, the majority of peasants were overjoyed to learn of
the fall of Robespierre and the dismantling of the political and economic
system of the Terror at the end of 1794. For the richer farmers in
particular 1795 was to prove an extremely lucrative year. Freed from
the restrictions of the Maximum, benefiting from rising grain prices
as a result of a disastrous harvest, the big farmer began to imitate the
style of life hitherto associated only with the urban bourgeoisie. In
the Pays de Caux district, 'their houses are well-furnished . . . their

wives and daughters decked with the finest jewellery. The old image of the peasant sitting by the fire-side drinking his bowl of thin soup is no longer valid'. The bitter hostility between rich and poor in the town aggravated by the worst famine in France since 1709, was not entirely absent in the countryside.

The famine of 1795, for all the immediate suffering it caused, did at least serve one useful purpose: it reminded the Government and the peasantry of their dependence on wheat as the basic unit of food production. The Revolution did not initiate any major changes either in the methods of cultivation or in the type of crops which the peasantry produced. Custom, collective rights and the complicated system of landholding in scattered strips outside the village all proved to be powerful brakes on agricultural improvement.

Marginal advances had been made in the course of the second half of the eighteenth century such as the introduction of root crops and fodder for animal stock, but, despite the prompting of the Physiocrats and the learned discourses delivered in hundreds of Academies, the vast majority of peasants continued to go about their labours in the time-honoured fashion. The shortage of cattle helps to

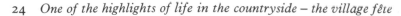

24   *One of the highlights of life in the countryside – the village fête*

explain why the land was allowed to lie fallow once in every three years, even in alternate years in many regions south of the Loire; few cattle meant little fertilisation and lack of fertilisation meant fallow land. In 1795, the Government introduced rice and potatoes to alleviate the widespread suffering caused by the shortage of grain, but the people had very little notion of how to prepare rice, and they still regarded the potato as fit only for their pigs.

It was only under Napoleon who, like the Physiocrats, considered agriculture to be the primary source of wealth, that important, although still limited, advances were made. In a few South-Eastern departments maize was introduced to offset the traditional dependence on wheat and the potato was seen more frequently, although only reluctantly, on the peasant's table. As a result of Napoleon's continental blockade and the loss of France's colonies, an attempt was made to introduce new crops like chicory, sugar beet, tobacco and cotton. Promoted by the Prefects and various Ministers of Agriculture, the majority of these laudable schemes foundered on the resistance of the soil, the climate and the peasantry. The production of sugar-beet, however, might be termed a qualified success: by 1815 there were approximately 500 sugar-refining plants in France. Artificial fertilisers began to make their appearance on the most efficient farms. Although it is clear that these changes in cultivation and variation of crops only affected a small sector of the agricultural economy there is little doubt that they did mitigate the worst effects of the bad harvest of 1812. It was to be a long time, however, before French agriculture overcame the drawbacks of outmoded techniques, the lack of adequate credit facilities and the absence of a truly national market.

Apart from a relatively small number of affluent farmers, the style of life which characterised peasant society did not undergo any appreciable change during the Revolution and Empire.

Throughout our period the fear of famine continued to haunt the minds of both the peasantry and the government. The poor harvests of 1788–89 had precipitated a revolutionary crisis and unleashed the Great Fear in the countryside; the terrible famine of 1795 provoked the abortive risings of the spring of that year in Paris and, not only in the capital but throughout France, brought disease, a high rate of suicide and widespread starvation. In 1812 the Malet

25   *A town market-place in late eighteenth-century France*

conspiracy to overthrow Napoleon was not unrelated to the serious economic situation which was partly to be explained by yet another poor harvest. Famine increased the antagonism between town and countryside. The peasant, always reluctant to see grain convoys leaving his locality, was understandably more hostile during a period of scarcity. For the villagers around the capital it was particularly galling to know that bread was being sold more cheaply in the city itself but that, owing to police regulations, it was impossible (or at least difficult) to smuggle the precious commodity through the custom-posts back to one's home. Dearth exaggerated the historic provincialism of French life: it set the landless against the land-owning peasant; it awakened old animosities against the neighbouring province, against the nearest town and, most of all, against Paris. In the eyes of the average peasant, the town-dweller was living off the fat of the land which he had to cultivate.

The response of the authorities to the threat of famine did not alter substantially before 1815. Increasingly laissez-faire in principle, governments, whether Monarchist, Jacobin or Napoleonic, invariably introduced the traditional mechanism of price-fixing and requisition in a crisis. Bread riots were to pose the most serious challenge to governments until the 1830s. The introduction of price-fixing laws had to be considered very carefully: too much constraint might provoke the very panic and fears which governments were most anxious to avoid. In addition, the peasantry, or at least rural producers, were bitterly opposed to such regulations. During the famine of 1812 the Prefect of the Aveyron, echoing the sentiments of the farmers in his department, told the Government in no uncertain terms that, 'Price-fixing is a disastrous, unjust and impractical measure . . . in that it imposes on the profits of the farmer restrictions which are not placed on other producers . . .'.

However, since urban and rural consumers depended almost entirely on bread for their daily subsistence, governments could afford to ignore rising prices in other non-essential sectors of the economy. As one leading Physiocrat of the eighteenth century had explained: 'I am all for freedom of trade, but bread is a matter for the police.' Until such time as improvements in agricultural yields and techniques and an increased volume of trade and industry produced a more varied diet and a wider market, governments tended to sympathise with this view. Their main problem, as the Jacobins found, was that they did not possess the bureaucratic and administrative personnel necessary to make the application of such regulations effective.

Confronted with a crisis, governments usually relied on the well-proven device of setting up soup-kitchens and workshops. *Ateliers de charité* were created in 1789 and again, in certain regions, in 1795. The Napoleonic régime, far better equipped from an administrative point of view, ran the system most effectively in 1812. During the winter months, according to a report by the Prefect of the Gard, women and children had been picking weeds and roots to eat, 'not', according to the Prefect, 'a completely disagreeable source of nourishment'! At the peak of the crisis in March 1812 no fewer than 89,407 individuals in the Gard alone were kept alive on bowls of soup made from rice and peas. Of course, the recipients of such charity were expected to express their gratitude in a practical way, either by weaving, spinning, or digging roads and ditches. The limited amount of food kept the mass of the population from starvation; hard labour ensured that what little energy the people still possessed would not be used for rioting. The Napoleonic régime avoided massive unrest in 1812 by maintaining a very fine balance between the provision of soup and the shovel.

Begging and brigandage were the natural heirs to famine in the eighteenth century. Both these forms of 'anti-social' behaviour had a long and, from the standpoint of criminality, dishonourable tradition in peasant societies. Highwaymen, salt-smugglers, child-beggars, bands of outlaws like the *Chauffeurs du Nord* are to be found as stock characters in eighteenth-century literature. The rise in population after 1750 made it even more difficult for the peasant to provide for his wife and children. In a famine year, the sons and daughters of day-labourers had no other recourse than to set out for the towns or scour the countryside in search of food and shelter. It was from 1795 to 1799 that the worst period of anarchy in the countryside occurred, although as late as 1812 reports from various local authorities speak of 'armies of beggars' plaguing the more affluent farmers for food and work. This perennial problem was made more acute during the last few years of the eighteenth century by the severity of the economic crisis of 1795–6, the social and political dislocation occasioned by the Revolution and the massive scale of desertion from the Republican armies. In 1797, a Government Commission urged greater severity to counteract 'the multiplicity, the audacity and the cruelty' of acts of brigandage: two years later yet another Commission begged the Government to find some answer to deal with 'le torrent des assassinats'.

It was in Southern France, where religious differences were super-imposed on economic and political antagonisms and where the pattern of violence assumed a unique and extreme form, that brigandage was most widespread after 1795. Gangs of Catholic Royalists, like the *Compagnies du soleil* around Lyons, or, more simply, *les fanatiques* around Nîmes, accounted for hundreds of victims chosen principally on political grounds, although the distinction between political and personal crimes was always confused. A report of 1799 stated that many acts of violence in the countryside had been committed against 'public officials, owners of National Lands and all those citizens attached to the Constitution of 1795'. Other bands of brigands directed their activities against the wealthier farmers whose rapacity and selfishness during the crisis of 1795 was well-documented in the popular mind. Some municipalities employed shepherds or *gardes champêtres* to protect crops and property but, badly paid and recruited from the most deprived sections of the community, they were frequently responsible for the very crimes they were supposed to prevent.

Smuggling, another traditional pursuit, reached even more professional heights during the Napoleonic period as a result of the embargo on foreign imports: just as, under the *ancien régime*, entire villages had derived their livelihood from smuggling salt from one province to another, so, under Napoleon, thousands of fishermen, peasants and rural artisans involved themselves in the contraband trade. Smugglers, poachers, brigands, the underworld of rural societies, often protected by the respectable who were not above profiting from their crimes, formed an essential part of life in the countryside.

To deal with these groups, and the deserters whose numbers increased substantially after 1812, Napoleon would have needed the Grande Armée itself. For peasants living in lonely and remote farm-houses, fear of 'les brigands' was real and understandable. The threat of arson was always used, as it had been since time immemorial, to give greater force to their demands. Arson was a traditional form of protest in the countryside: it was not uncommon to hear some villager remark that one of his enemies 'deserved to be grilled like a pig over a fire'. Nor was it unknown for a small-holder, forced off his farm as a result of his debts, to set fire to his barn or even his cottage in order to prevent the property passing into the hands of a rival. The *chauffeurs* derived their name from the practice of 'warming' the soles of victims' feet in order to obtain information of hidden sources of wealth.

The Revolution had emancipated the peasantry from the social, economic and juridical restrictions of a decaying feudal system. It had provided, principally for the more affluent, an opportunity of acquiring property as a result of the sale of Church and émigré lands; it had also meant the assignat, the Maximum, dechristianisation and, particularly between 1795 and 1799, a situation bordering upon anarchy in many provinces. Social antagonism within the peasant community itself had been increased and little or nothing had been done for the share-cropper and the landless labourer.

The Napoleonic régime did ensure that the Church and the aristocracy would never again exert, at least from an economic and legal standpoint, the same authority over the peasants. It had also restored the Catholic and Protestant cults, and mitigated the worst effects of famine by virtue of a more efficient administrative system and better cultivation. However, the Empire had created an army of petty officials —the *commissaire de police*, the customs officer, the tax assessor and, perhaps most important of all, the recruiting-sergeant. Many peasants must have wondered if freedom from feudalism had been bought at too high a price.

4   'Careers Open to Talents'

The term 'bourgeois revolution', referring to the events of 1789, tends to obscure as much of the truth as it reveals. The crisis of 1789 was, in fact, precipitated by the aristocracy; the peasantry and, in particular, the Parisian lower classes, provided the continued momentum. It has been argued that the Revolution actually retarded the pace of industrial growth. Certainly it is true that agricultural and industrial production did not accelerate along a broad front; that there was no marked exodus from the countryside to the towns; that the peasant proprietor had carved out a more secure niche for himself by 1815 than he had enjoyed in 1789. It is also true that social customs and patterns of behaviour, formed over centuries, are not lightly overthrown even by upheavals on the scale of the Revolution. Nevertheless by rationalising and modernising administrative, legal, economic and political institutions, by reducing the prestige—if not the pretensions—of the aristocracy and by reinforcing the relationship between political power and wealth, the Revolution undoubtedly broadened the avenues of advancement to the middle classes.

The word 'bourgeois' originally designated an inhabitant of a *bourg* or town. Under the *ancien régime* towns continued to possess their own privileges—exemption from the *taille*, the *corvée* or military service as in the case of Orleans. In 1789 the word did not carry with it any of the pejorative connotations added in the course of the nineteenth century: it referred to a man of substance usually living off his income from commerce, manufacture, pensions or rents. Adrien Duport, a leading member of the Constituent Assembly, described the bourgeoisie as, 'that entire class of men who live on wealth acquired from the profits of a skill or productive trade which they have accumulated themselves or inherited from their parents; finally those, always excepting the nobility, who have an income which is not dependent upon the work of their own hands'. It was the rise of this 'class' which altered the balance of social forces in eighteenth-century

France. As another deputy, Barnave, explained: 'Just as the possession of land elevated the aristocracy, so industrial and personal property elevates the power of the people' ('people' being a more acceptable term in 1789 than the bourgeoisie).

The increased prosperity of the commercial and industrial classes in eighteenth-century France is hardly open to question. The colonial trade with the Antilles, especially Santo Domingo, laid the basis for the visible wealth of the towns along the western seaboard. Representing one-quarter of the total export trade in 1715, this lucrative commerce with the colonies accounted for almost one-half by 1789. Nantes developed along much the same lines as Liverpool, its prosperity founded on those two much-coveted commodities, sugar and slaves. In 1700, 40,000 slaves had been transported to the Antilles; by 1784 this figure had passed the half million mark. Production of manufactured articles more than tripled during the course of the eighteenth century; cotton more than doubled in the same period; coal production increased five-fold from 1750 to 1775; cast-iron by seventy per cent between 1738 and 1789. A few steam-engines made their belated appearance in the bigger concerns like the Anzin mines which employed over 4,000 workers. De Wendel in Lorraine and Dollfuss in Mulhouse were adopting English techniques and skilled workers. Paris was the international centre for the luxury trade; Lyons for the silk and textile industries.

There was, however, no important technological change in the industrial sector; increased production occurred within the old framework. Roads were still bad, particularly in the East; the road from Lille to Arras was pitted with ruts three feet deep and the journey from Paris to Calais had to be done in twenty-six stages. At the end of the eighteenth century an average of only 200 stage-coaches a day left the capital taking over ten days to reach Milan. Anything over seventy miles was considered a good day's travelling.

The accession to the throne of Louis XVI in 1774 coincided with a prolonged period of economic stagnation. Textile manufacturers were adversely affected by the terms of the Eden Treaty with England in 1786. Large factories were the exception rather than the rule, the basic unit of production being the master-craftsman employing a dozen or fewer workers in the towns, or a peasant family in the countryside finishing off goods for an entrepreneur. French industry was still very regional in character, and the multiplicity of guilds, corporations, toll-charges on roads and water-ways, custom-posts, and government regulations acted as powerful brakes on capitalist incentive and enterprise.

Even before the Revolution some effort had been made to overcome these obstacles. The number of guilds had been reduced in 1776 from over a hundred to forty-four. Many manufacturers promoted the disintegration of the medieval institutions protecting the rights and privileges of skilled craftsmen. In the South-East, Protestant silk-merchants sought 'to create a separate corps for themselves in order to distinguish the merchants from the master-craftsmen whom they seek to reduce to the status of ordinary workers'. Nor was the entrepreneurial spirit entirely absent. In the Grande-Combe region, destined to be one of the most productive coal-producing areas in France, the Tubeuf family was endeavouring in the 1780s to concentrate the small mines which pockmarked the hills into one profit-making concern, but was forced to contend with bitter opposition, not only from the local miners, but from vested aristocratic interests including no less a figure than the marquis de Castries, Louis XVI's Minister of the Marine. Tubeuf himself, a little discouraged, decided to emigrate to the New World where he encountered even stronger resistance—he was killed by Red Indians in Virginia!

If one accepts the term 'bourgeois revolution' as a useful generalisation, it remains true that for particular sections of the middle classes the Revolution proved to be a disaster. This was the case for those who had invested heavily in seigneurial estates and titles; for the large rentier class living off fixed incomes and pensions; for the merchants engaged in the colonial trade who tended to look back to the days of Louis XVI with nostalgia as, one by one, France lost most of her colonies; and for the manufacturers of some luxury goods who found revolutionary austerity rather trying on their pockets, whatever good it may have done their souls. Since social and economic differences amongst the bourgeoisie were so marked one can hardly expect to find any united front being presented to the Revolution.

There were few complaints, however, from one section of the bourgeoisie—war-contractors, bankers and speculators. Particularly

26   *The fashionable Boulevard des Italiens in the spring of 1797*

after the fall of Robespierrre (whose incorruptibility bordered on the boring), these nouveaux-riches succeeded in amassing vast fortunes out of supplying the armies, loans to successive régimes, and property-deals. Perrégaux, of Swiss origin like so many bankers of the time, acquired his vast fortune from banking and supplying grain to the Army. Since he made so much money out of the Revolution, one should not be surprised to see Perrégaux doing his National Guard duty in 1789 or keeping the Committee of Public Safety afloat, financially, in 1794. He was to be one of the first Regents of the Bank of France created by Napoleon in 1800. Claude Perier, a merchant from Grenoble, opened a bank in Paris in 1793 and went on to involve himself in most of the speculative ventures afforded by the Revolution. His son was to become Prime Minister under the July Monarchy.

Like Perier, Ouvrard did not confine himself to banking. In 1794, according to his own testimony, he made 500,000 francs in three months out of the colonial trade. A few years later, he was in a position to finance the Directory to the tune of ten million francs. Ouvrard lived in splendour with the customary *hotél* in Paris and several chateaux in the provinces. Colombier-Batteur opened a clothing-store to supply the *armée de Hollande* and by shrewd investments out of the proceeds made himself a millionaire by 1817. Napoleon Bonaparte was obliged to rely upon such men to finance his costly war-machine although he was not above biting the hands that fed him. In 1806 Ouvrard suffered the indignity of a spell inside the Emperor's prison for his part in speculating against the Bank of France. The firm of Flachat-Laporte and Castelin was described by Napoleon as 'the greatest crooks in Europe'.

The period also offered considerable possibilities to the relatively small number of wealthy merchants and industrialists. If the Atlantic and Mediterranean ports suffered as a result of the Revolution, cities like Strasbourg, Lyons and Paris benefited. The abolition of the guilds, repressive legislation like the Loi Chapelier in 1791 which forbade strikes and coalitions for higher wages, the disappearance of many internal customs and tolls, a unified system of weights and measures and the introduction of the decimal system in 1803 obviously created a new ethos in which certain sectors of the industrial and commercial world could expand. War, the continental blockade and indifferent means of communication did not prevent men like Delessert from making considerable profits by refining sugar beet. Oberkampf's success in producing some of the finest printed cloths of the time won him the Légion d'Honneur. Napoleon took a keen interest in industry, providing considerable sums of money to encourage new inventions like Jacquard's loom which was to revolutionise the production of silk, and creating such institutions as the *Société d'encouragement pour l'industrie nationale* in 1801.

From a purely political point of view, however, it was the professional, or 'legal and literate' bourgeoisie who played the most significant role in the Revolution. The growth of literacy, the use of the printed word, the theatre and other channels of communication all served to bring the events of 1789 to the attention of a fairly wide audience. *Ancien régime* government and society, with its complex legal system buttressed by thousands of manorial courts, its unwieldy fiscal and bureaucratic apparatus, had offered employment to thousands of lawyers and office-holders. Angers, a town of just over 30,000 inhabitants, boasted no fewer than fifty-three law courts; *avocats, notaires* and *officiers* represented a sizeable proportion of the middle-class populations of towns like Rennes, Toulouse and Grenoble, to say nothing of the capital. *Notaires* were particularly important, advising clients on a whole range of problems, acting as middlemen for merchants and landowners, settling property disputes, dealing with wills and investments. This group provided the Revolution with its leading political cadres. The majority of deputies in the early revolutionary assemblies were drawn from the ranks of the lawyers and office-holders. Napoleon, who, when he was not engaged on the battlefield, devoted the greater part of his time to codifying every aspect of French life, was forced to rely heavily on this same class. The Emperor feared their influence, describing them, with considerable justification, as 'artisans des révolutions'.

Other professional groups like teachers, scientists and, to a lesser degree, doctors also exerted an influence disproportionate to their numerical strength. There was an increasing demand among the more cultured and literate section of the population for information on the important scientific discoveries of the age. Auguste Comte, one of the founders of the modern discipline of sociology, wrote in 1803 that 'mankind's one true common interest lies in the progress of the sciences'. The discoveries of the seventeenth and eighteenth centuries, popularised by such influential writers as Voltaire and Diderot, provides the essential background to the work of Lagrange and Monge in mathematics, Berthollet and Fourcroy in chemistry, Coulomb and Ampère in physics. In the field of biology, Lamarck was foreshadowing Darwin by stressing the influence of environment on the modification of all life-forms. Scientists were given a place of honour in the famous *Institut*; the Ecole Polytechnique, the Jardin du Roi and the Conservatoire des Arts et Métiers provided the avenues through which the new discoveries and ideas could be transmitted to a wider public. There are echoes of the Renaissance in the Catholic response to artistic and scientific achievement in this period. Napoleon was conscious of this fact and leading scientists like Chaptal and Fourcroy were given important posts in his administration. Like most apolitical regimes the Empire relied heavily on technocrats and businessmen.

The status of doctors also underwent a perceptible change from 1789 to 1815. The experience gained, and the respect earned, by the medical profession in a period of almost continuous warfare clearly had repercussions on civilian life. Legislation was passed during the early years of the Revolution conferring the rank of officer on army doctors; blue-prints were drawn up for new medical schools, although far too little was actually achieved. It proved difficult to overcome the traditional prejudice against surgeons who were regarded, often quite justifiably, as ill-trained practitioners of a trade which alternated between cutting hair and amputating limbs. Physicians were treated with far greater deference, although when one considers the treatment they administered one tends to be more than a little surprised. The most customary remedy for all kinds of ailments continued to be blood-letting in some form or other, whether by opening veins or by applying leeches. Madame Hummel, wife of a well-to-do merchant in Nantes— probably suffering from cancer—was advised by her physician to place a raw egg on her stomach in order to relieve the condition. Little wonder

27 *Jenner's anti-smallpox vaccine did not gain immediate acceptance from the public!*

28   *The 'Dandies of the Directory' reflect the more uninhibited society
of post-Jacobin France*

that in 1798 there were 'protests everywhere against the quackery and
incompetence that endangered the health and lives of the citizenry'.

Despite Napoleon's distrust of doctors (like lawyers they tended to
think too much), the study and practice of medicine did improve under
the Empire. The drastic reduction of the army medical corps by
Napoleon proved to be a blessing for the civilian community. By 1815,
Paris was becoming renowned as a centre for the study of clinical
medicine. The work of such professors as Pinel and Thouret heralded a
new era in the medical field. The stethoscope made its first appearance.
Jenner's vaccine against smallpox, despite initial difficulties and the
bitter scorn and hostility of the majority of physicians, was being used
fairly extensively by 1815, thus eliminating one of the greatest scourges
of *ancien régime* society.

No simple generalisations could possibly reflect the varying status
and reactions of those bourgeois who did not fall into either the professional or the commercial and manufacturing classes—the rentier
class, which formed such a high percentage of the middle-class population and who were adversely affected by the inflation of the 1790s;
the master-craftsmen, amongst whom there were those whose livelihood

depended ultimately, as in Lyons or Nîmes, upon the merchant-manufacturers who provided them with raw materials and then organised the sale and distribution of the finished goods. The social status of this last group was declining although they still maintained the pretensions and attitudes which raised them above the level of ordinary workers. Then there were the independent craftsmen, especially in Paris, such as jewellers, goldsmiths, cabinet-makers, small contractors and wholesale traders whose social and economic existence depended upon their own business acumen and skills. The large and extremely diverse world of the craftsman and shopkeeper inhabited a no-man's land between the *classes populaires* and the bourgeoisie and will be discussed in the following chapter.

The marked gradations of wealth and social status which distinguished one stratum of the population from another are reflected in their differing modes of life. The upper middle-classes, imbued with the new liberal ideas, sought both an end to the restrictions imposed by *ancien régime* society and the translation of their economic supremacy into social and political terms. Their ideal was the Constitution of 1791 which sanctified the right of property, introduced equality before the law, religious toleration, anti-working class legislation and the division of Frenchmen into 'active' and 'passive' citizens (based on tax qualifications). Their disdain for the less favoured of their fellow-citizens is indicated in a bourgeois petition of 1789 which described the inmates of the *ateliers de charité* at Montmartre (then outside the city limits) as, 'Truly a horde of savages at the door of the most civilised city in the world'. The manufacturers of printed fabrics, the wholesale merchants and owners of sugar-refineries in Orleans 'shared a certain way of life—respect for birth and wealth, a horror of bad marriages, arrogance towards small property-owners and contempt for the populace'.

If the division between town and country was evident during the Revolution there was also a sociological chasm between the bourgeois living within the city proper and the masses living outside the walls. When a proposal to pull down the medieval walls surrounding the city of Nîmes was made on the eve of the Revolution, one city-dweller objected on the grounds that if this was done the city would be threatened 'by the violence of the people living in the faubourgs, five-eighths of whom were prone to thieving, pillaging, murder and lewdness'.

Wealthy bourgeois like the bankers Sequin and Ouvrard lived in the grand manner. Surrounded by a regiment of valets, footmen, cooks and maids, throwing sumptuous banquets and soirées, patronising the arts (no fashionable mansion was complete without its picture gallery), their style of life confirmed the rise of the new aristocracy of wealth. Madame Divoff, invited to a party at the home of the banker Geller situated in the Chaussée d'Antin, commented: 'His house was truly of the most astonishing splendour ... Never, in any country, have I seen such magnificence, even among seigneurs.' Ouvrard's cosy retreat in the chateau de Raincy (in addition to one's town house, it was important to have a summer residence in Raincy, Neuilly or Clichy) was furnished in accordance with the current vogue for the colossal and the classical with mythological figures and motifs and an enormous bathroom built in marble and granite. Madame Récamier, wife of a rich banker, designed her mansion in much the same way with heavy, gilded tables and cabinets. One climbed onto her white-muslin draped bed (and it was whispered that many did) only after ascending a series of cedar-wood steps. Cabinet-makers like the famous Jacob brothers, sculptors in bronze like Denière, goldsmiths and jewellers, all found a new clientele to replace, or rather to complement, their former noble patrons.

If Robespierre had lodged quite simply, but very comfortably with the Duplay family, subsequent ministers and dignitaries failed to emulate his frugal way of life. Barras organised lavish *fêtes* in the Luxembourg gardens, and an invitation from Napoleon's Arch-Chancellor, Cambacérès, usually involved a two-hour feast complete with the choicest and most varied cuisine. The French have long been renowned for their culinary arts, but at no time in recent history were gastronomic pleasures taken more seriously than under the Directory and Empire. Grimod de la Reynière, the acknowledged master, even decided to publish an *Almanach des Gourmands*. Scores of new restaurants opened around the turn of the century offering the best in provincial and international cuisine. One of the most famous in Paris, Very's, provided a bill of fare which included twenty-five hors d'oeuvres, thirty-one entrées of game, twenty-eight veal and mutton dishes, to say nothing of the multiplicity of pastries, cheeses and an admirable selections of wines.

Having wined and dined at Very's, Paris offered a wealth of entertainment for the more enterprising of the bourgeoisie. One could be seen, *en famille*, walking along the fashionable areas of the Champs Elysées, the Bois de Boulogne or the Tuileries gardens, or one could arrange a picnic at St Cloud. Many preferred to mingle with the crowd in the delightfully landscaped gardens of Frascati's or Tivoli's where one could watch magnificent firework displays or sit and enjoy an iced drink or a glass of chocolate. The exploits of famous balloonists like Garnerin and Blanchard excited the imagination of all France: on 2 October 1798, Testu-Brissy was lifted into the clouds on horseback! The bourgeoisie patronised the official theatres—the Opéra and the Comédie-Française—or, if they preferred to go slumming, the many boulevard theatres which specialised in puppet-shows, pantomimes and melodramas. Perhaps the most popular diversion of all was to stroll through the Palais Royal: 'Quel monde', exclaimed Madame Divoff

29 *Coachmen plying their trade for popular 'day-trips' to the rural outskirts of Paris*

30　*The exploits of 'aeronauts' like Garnerin attracted almost as much publicity as present-day astronauts*

after her first visit, 'What shops, what cafés and restaurants. One could spend one's entire life in the Palais Royal enjoying every conceivable kind of entertainment and amusement. One can purchase one's clothes, find somewhere to dine, stroll at leisure through the arcades, then visit a theatre. Really, in my opinion, it's a perfect paradise.' Madame Divoff, true to her good breeding, omitted to mention that the Palais Royal was also the favourite haunt of prostitutes.

31　*Prostitution was an essential part of Parisian society under the Directory*

Outside the fashionable areas like the faubourg Saint-Honoré and the Chaussée d'Antin, the Parisian bourgeoisie lived fairly unostentatiously. Until well into the nineteenth century the middle and lower classes were not entirely separated geographically in the bigger cities. Although the 'perpendicular' nature of social status in revolutionary Paris—the higher up the appartment block one lived the lower one's station in life—has probably been exaggerated, the fact that employers and employees often lived, ate and slept under the same roof did mean that workers were imbued with middle-class values and attitudes.

The lower bourgeoisie resented the arrogance of the rich almost as much as they feared the violence of the poor. Madame Miotte, whose husband earned 5,000 livres a year, had only one servant and did most of her own cooking. As a concession to prevailing tastes, however, her gilt clock was classical in style. Madame Hummel lived in a modest house, although she maintained four servants. Her account-book provides a valuable picture of what it must have been like to run a bourgeois household during a period of tremendous inflation. In

1790, a pound of sugar cost just 18 sous, a bushel of flour two livres; by 1795, with the assignat practically worthless, the same commodities cost 62 and 225 livres respectively. According to one of her last entries, a sack of potatoes cost her 17,000 livres! At this point, not having been trained in higher mathematics, Madame admitted defeat and closed her book.

The Terror of 1793–4 did send shivers of apprehension up the spines of the well-to-do, or at least of those who were either silly or high-principled enough to profess the cardinal crime of 'indifference' to the Popular Movement. The occasional desire expressed by the more sanguine of the 'mob' that they 'would like to eat the head of a bourgeois', was hardly calculated to allay such fears. Nevertheless, domestic life did not come to a halt even as the tumbrils trundled along to the Place de Grève. At the beginning of 1794, Madame Julien's daughter went off to her piano lessons in the morning and returned to face the memorisation of set passages from Racine and Corneille. The theatres were doing a booming trade. On one occasion the entire Julien household, including the cook, went off to see the great Talma in one of the most notable of his performances, that of Nero. Mareux, a manufacturer of mirrors and subsequently owner of a theatre, found himself thrust reluctantly into politics as a member of the Paris Commune, but was soon back struggling, rather unsuccess-fully, to make a living out of his theatre. And if the middle classes had suffered during the Year II of the Republic, more from the insolence of the *petit peuple* than the threat of physical violence, they had to wait but a short time before the Thermidorean regime which replaced the rule of the Jacobins and lasted from 1794 to 1795 gave them an opportunity for revenge.

One could usually recognise a bourgeois by his dress. During the early years of the Revolution, fashions changed from the more extravagant attire of the *ancien régime* to the more neutral costume of the frock-coat, breeches, black stockings and gloves with a muslin cravat. By 1793, few deputies copied Robespierre's unrepentant bourgeois dress complete with powdered wig. It was not until the Directory that all restraints were cast off, the ladies appearing in high-waisted and very décolleté dresses of silk, muslin, even of gauze.

There were of course extremes in taste—the *muscadins* with their

32 *Extracting teeth was a painful process, almost as painful as winning over royalists to the Republic*

tight breeches, voluminous coats, silk-stockings and pointed shoes; the *Incroyables*, similarly attired but with the distinguishing rustic stick and two-cornered hat; the *merveilleuses*, with their Grecian tunics, who developed the art 'of knowing how to hide nothing whilst at the same time appearing to be fully-dressed', changed their wigs every four hours and their conversation to match. The letter 'r' disappeared from their vocabulary—'ma pa'ole sup'ème', 'c'est ho'ible', an affectation not confined entirely to this bizarre period. Classical styles continued to predominate during the Napoleonic period with dresses à la Cérès, sandals à la Psyche, hats and hair-styles in the Grecian fashion. There was, however, far less immodesty: the ladies in particular were fitted into the Napoleonic straight-jacket with the reappearance of the corset.

Women played an important role in the Revolution, either by prompting their husbands or admirers to man the barricades or by taking the lead themselves for example during the March from Paris to Versailles which led to the return of the royal family to the capital, in October 1789. There were also some females like the actress Claire Lacombe or the more flamboyant Théroigne de Méricourt, an imposing figure in her Henry IV hat, sans-culotte costume and long sword, who

33   *The influence of classical Rome was all too visible in Napoleonic France*

were active in their pursuit of female emancipation and who were certainly 'politically aware'. In general, however, the popular classes shared with the bourgeoisie a common disdain for the woman who left her washing, her stove or her children to participate in politics. Under the Directory, it was in the home, at the theatre, or in the salons that women found their true role.

Led by the beautiful Madame Récamier (the best advertisement for her husband's bank) and Madame Tallien, polite society began to find an outlet for its desires. The nouveaux-riches met at the Tallien's, occasionally at the official salons of Talleyrand or Cambacérès. The old and the new élites could often be found in the salons of Madame Junot, or Madame de Rémusat. It was in these select circles that one could listen to the great singers of the day, Garat or 'la Grassini', watch the great dancer Vestris perform or listen to Chateaubriand pretentiously intone his latest chef-d'oeuvre. For those who stood a little beneath this elevated rank there were numerous public or private balls where one could indulge in the craze for dancing the quadrille, the waltz or the mazurka. Gaming rivalled dancing as the favourite pastime of the wealthy under the Empire. In Paris and the provinces hundreds of establishments, mostly under private auspices, offered an

34   *(Overleaf) In this print even the animals are swept along by the contemporary craze for dancing*

35   *Gaming rivalled dancing as the most popular pastime during the Empire*

avenue of escape for those who agreed with Madame de Stael that France, under Napoleon, 'was a garrison where military discipline and boredom rule'.

Despite the fact that certain writers like the literary critic Geoffroy were known to bemoan the 'monopolisation of revolutionary freedom by women and children', and possibly even the influence of Rousseau's *Emile* in creating a more natural home environment for the young, the place of women in French society was modified rather than transformed by the Revolution. There was a certain degree of emancipation. The institution of civil marriage and divorce in September 1792 was obviously a powerful factor in this direction: in 1800, 698 divorces were recorded in the capital for 3,215 marriages. Napoleon's Civil Code, however, rescinded much of the liberal legislation of the early years of the Revolution. Divorce laws were made more stringent; adultery was once again regarded as a heinous crime for women, but little more than an example of human weakness in the male of the species; the authority of the father concerning, for example, the disposition of family property was reinstated. It was, of course to be another 130 years before women were given the privilege to vote.

If social mobility increased during the Revolution and Empire, favouring the triumph of wealth over birth, the bourgeoisie, who were best qualified to exploit such opportunities, tended to express their new freedom in traditional ways. Although, in social terms, the middle classes followed different modes of life in accordance with their wealth and position, they were at least united in one thing—the acquisition of property. All French constitutions in this period stressed the sanctity of property. Although statistics on the purchase of National Lands are still surprisingly inadequate, those that exist suggest that in most regions it was the bourgeoisie who acquired the lion's share.

In parts of the Nord, they owned almost one-third of the land by 1804 as opposed to just under one-sixth in 1789; in the department of the Cher, their investment was four times that of the peasantry; 'everywhere in southern Anjou, the bourgeois were the principal beneficiaries

36   *A satirical comment on the tight dresses and loose morals*
of Napoleonic France

of the sales of church property . . . in the Mauges, their predominance was overwhelming'. As under the *ancien régime*, land continued to be the most attractive form of investment for all but the dedicated entrepreneur. Throughout the nineteenth century the middle classes exhibited a similar reluctance to embark upon risky business ventures, preferring to sink their money into an estate in the provinces than a coal-mine in the North-East. In this respect, the objectives of the bourgeoisie were conditioned by the *ancien régime*; their attainment was facilitated by the Revolution.

In 1799 the majority of the middle classes had welcomed the rise to power of Napoleon Bonaparte in order to protect what they had acquired during the early years of the Revolution. For over a decade Napoleon satisfied most of their demands. The Civil Code confirmed their seizure of National Lands, equality before the law and the principle of religious toleration; the expansion of the French Imperium to include Belgium, Holland, Italy, Switzerland, parts of Germany and for a brief period, Spain, offered an expanding market for the manufacturing and industrial middle class, to say nothing of the possibilities for advancement offered to the sons of the bourgeoisie in the army and an ever-increasing bureaucracy. Although a small minority of ideologues chafed against the loss of political freedom the great majority of bourgeois appeared to be well satisfied with 'le petit corporal'.

Opinion began to change after the first decade of Napoleonic rule. It was not so much that the bourgeoisie grew tired of the war, more that they regretted the consequences of being defeated in war. The effects of the English blockade, and the closure of one continental market after another, culminated in a period of contraction, if not stagnation, in trade and industry. The silk and textile industries found it impossible to obtain an outlet for their goods: in the South-East, the total value of articles sold at the international fair of Beaucaire fell by almost a half between 1806 and 1811. The Atlantic and Mediterranean ports, already suffering from the loss of the colonial trade, were seriously affected by the depression. The defeat of the *Grande Armée* in 1812, coupled with the disastrous harvest of that year, reduced support for Napoleon amongst all classes. Louis XVIII may not have been the most popular of French kings, but he was certainly preferable to a military dictator who could no longer promise success on the battlefield.

In any case, the Constitutional Charter which Louis XVIII was obliged to draw up before ascending the throne in 1814 held few terrors for the middle classes. Despite strong pressure from the émigrés, it confirmed the legality of their purchase of church and noble property and provided for a parliamentary as opposed to an absolutist régime. From a political and administrative point of view the middle classes were obliged to compete for the spoils of office with the aristocracy, but so far as economic power was concerned they had emerged triumphant from the Revolution. In 1791, the popular journalist Marat had written: 'What will it benefit us to destroy the aristocracy of birth if it is going to be replaced by an aristocracy of wealth?' If indeed he had been speaking on behalf of the lower orders, and had he lived to see the return of the Bourbons in 1814, he would surely have been aware that the dangers he had foreseen had in fact been realised.

5 The Revolution and the Classes Populaires

In the summer of 1789, again in 1792 and 1793, it was the Parisian *classes populaires*—the workshop-master, the apprentice, the inn-keeper, the butcher, the building-worker, the shop-keeper, assisted spasmodically by the colourful, often violent and occasionally criminal, floating population of the capital—which impelled the Revolution forward and towards more radical objectives. Regarded with suspicion and fear under the *ancien régime*, treated alternately with remarkable indulgence and brutal repression by the authorities, the Revolution afforded them one intoxicating moment of uncertain glory during the Terror of the Year II before they were once again relegated to their traditional role as consumers of bread, as mere cogs in an economic system which, from a technological point of view, was more medieval than modern.

Cities and towns at the end of the eighteenth century bore little resemblance to the sprawling conurbations of today. The urban population of France in 1815 accounted for less than fifteen per cent of the total population. In the big textile centre of Saint Etienne, there were 23,000 workers making ribbons and other articles on 12,000 looms—hardly the streamlined production methods of the twentieth century. There were of course factories, even in Paris which employed 200, 500, even 800 workers, but they tended to be exceptions rather than the rule. The basic unit of production was still the small workshop.

Most cities and towns retained their medieval aspect, dominated by spires and domes, with their traditional over-crowded *quartiers* and streets whose names denoted the economic interests of their inhabitants—rue de l'Horloge, rue des Halles, quai des Orfèvries or the rue du Vert-bois, a poignant reminder of medieval Paris, although, even during the Revolution, one could find gardens close to the centre of the city and it was not uncommon for people to keep chickens in their apartments.

Some of the wealthiest cities were to be found along the western coast-line. Ports like Bordeaux had experienced a notable boom during the eighteenth century; its fashionable areas, its theatres and its shops reflected this recent prosperity. Like Bordeaux, Rouen had grown rich on the colonial trade, although in neither city did the population reach 100,000 inhabitants. Lyons, the second city of the realm, could boast of only 150,000, Marseilles had just over 100,000, whilst in towns like Lille, Toulon and Nantes the population was about half this figure.

In matters of demography, as in practically every other sphere, Paris dominated the rest of France. With its population of approximately 650,000, most of the inhabitants crowded into the old faubourgs around the Cité and on both banks of the Seine. The capital was not simply the administrative, judicial and economic heart of France, it also laid well-founded claims to being the cultural capital of the Western world. No fashionable Grand Tour was complete without a lengthy stay in Paris. It was in its theatres, salons, restaurants and gambling-houses that the nobility of England, Germany and Russia congregated, their social intercourse facilitated by their acceptance of French as a common language. It was in Paris that singers and actors found fame, Swiss bankers made their fortunes and thousands of foreigners and provincials embarked upon the journey that would bring them, if not fame and wealth, then certainly the excitement of living in the great city. Yet not every visitor was impressed with his first sight of the capital: Jean-Jacques Rousseau entered the city through the faubourg Saint-Marcel and saw 'nothing but, dirty, stinking little streets, ugly black houses, a general air of squalor and poverty, beggars, carters, menders of clothes, sellers of herbal-drinks and old hats'.

Paris had grown considerably in size since Jean-Jacques' first visit half a century before the Revolution, stretching out like the tentacles of a huge starfish along the great roads which pointed the way to the four corners of France. However, the faubourgs in the heart of the city where, in the Year II, the Popular Movement had its geographic base, had not substantially changed. Along the Left Bank of the Seine, crowded with wage-earners who experienced the misery of the famine years more acutely than any other group, 70,000 Parisians made their homes; along the Right Bank lay the less densely-populated but politically more active faubourgs like Saint-Antoine and, still one of the most miserable parts of the city, the faubourg Saint-Marcel. According to Mercier, 'more money could be found in one house in the faubourg Saint-Honoré than in the entire faubourg of Saint-Marcel'. The neighbouring faubourg Saint-Antoine, marginally more prosperous with its hundreds of small craftsmen and shopkeepers, was to prove one of the main recruiting grounds for most of the revolutionary *journées*.

The Ile de la Cité represented the cross-roads of revolutionary Paris. On this small historic island could be found some of the most skilled craftsmen in Europe—the jewellers, goldsmiths and watch-makers, whose glittering shops were threaded, like so many jewels, alongside some of the finest medieval and Renaissance architecture. On the Pont-Neuf, one of the bridges which linked the island to the faubourgs, police-spies watching for known criminals mingled with the crowd whilst street-vendors emitted their raucous shouts making the spot one of the noisiest in the whole of Paris.

It was here, from 1789 to 1795, that the drama of the Popular

37 *A placard displaying the indestructible spirit of the Republic*

38 *'The standard-bearer'. A romanticised image of the revolutionary depicted by the famous artist Boilly*

Movement, with the sans-culottes playing the leading roles, was to be enacted. It is impossible to understand the course taken by the Revolution in its formative years without reference to the rise and fall of the Parisian sans-culottes. A stranger in the capital during the turbulent year of 1793 would have recognised the true sans-culotte in the first instance by his appearance. He disdained to wear the *culotte* or breeches which distinguished the aristocrat or the upper middle-classes, preferring the trousers of the working-man. If he were on his way to a meeting of his local Popular Society he would probably be wearing his *bonnet rouge*, the red Cap of Liberty, and perhaps carrying that symbol of sans-culotte militancy, the pike. He would speak in the familiar form of the French language since all men were equal, brothers in the cause of the Revolution.

Un petit Souper, a la Parisiènne: ____ or ____ A Family of Sans Culotts refreshing, after the fatigues of the day.

39   *A savage commentary on what the word 'sans-culotte' meant to the British establishment, published only a fortnight after the September Massacres in Paris*

'A sans-culotte is some-one who goes everywhere on foot, who isn't loaded with money like the rest of you, but lives quite simply with his wife and children ... on the fourth or fifth floor ...' (The poorer workers tended to occupy the top floors and attics of appartment blocks). Momoro speaks of the sans-culotte coming home to his garret after a hard day's work, 'moistening his dry crust of bread with his tears'. Such descriptions, popularised at the time by the savage cartoons of Gillray and later by imaginative writers like Dickens, are evocative but misleading: the sans-culotte did not represent the poorest section of the urban crowd. Some were in fact poor; many did live in garrets or furnished rooms. But the militant sans-culottes, those who formed the élites of the Sections and the Popular Societies, were more often than not skilled workers and shopkeepers.

An analysis of the social composition of the various committees which formed the institutional framework of the sans-culotte movement in the Year II shows that of 343 members of the *comités civils*, 26·2 per cent lived off private incomes; of 454 members of the more popularly recruited *comités révolutionnaires*, over sixty per cent were either craftsmen or shopkeepers. There is evidence that at least a few of these militants provided work, directly or indirectly, for hundreds of wage-earners. As a social group they were anything but cohesive

40   *A* comité révolutionnaire *in session. The man on the left is presenting his revolutionary identity-card*

which is not surprising since the concept of 'class' in the Marxist sense of the term was conspicuously absent during the Revolution. The stand which various groups took on the major political events of the time was often dictated by personal vendettas, professional jealousies and varying degrees of literacy as well as by purely economic factors.

The diffuse nature of the sans-culottes as a social class helps to explain their confused and occasionally 'reactionary' economic objectives. They were against the rich: many sans-culottes saw the Revolution as a straightforward struggle between rich and poor. Hébert fulminated in the lurid pages of his *Père Duchesne* against 'the selfish rich', 'the idle rich' and 'the useless rich'. Yet some sans-culottes lived off private incomes; many were relatively well-to-do craftsmen and shopkeepers. In general, what the sans-culottes objected to was the parade of wealth; they were not opposed to the concept of private property. Ideally, each citizen should own one workshop, one shop or one small farm—the Jacobin picture of a community of small independent producers.

Confronted with a nascent industrial society involving the concentration of industry, the sans-culotte often reacted in a contradictory but violent manner. Small craftsmen, employing a handful of trained apprentices or day-labourers who often lived under the same roof and ate at the same table, feared that they might lose their independence and be depressed into the status of a factory proletariat. In their demands for fixed prices, particularly a maximum on the price of bread, the sans-culottes were looking back to the paternalistic economy of the *ancien régime*, not forward to the era of laissez-faire. Thus, for the Revolutionary Government of 1793–94, the problems it faced were not those connected with strikes or demands for higher wages, but the potentially explosive queue outside the baker's shop, and the demand for cheap but edible food.

Lacking cohesion as a class, traditional in their economic outlook, the sans-culottes discovered a brittle unity in their egalitarianism and their profound sense of commitment to the Revolution. The term 'aristocrat' by 1793 had embraced, not only people of noble birth, but financiers, bankers and even rich grocers. In the spring of 1794, citizen Caillau climbed onto the roof of a shed to deliver a speech in praise of pillage, pointing out 'that only those who owned anything had reason to be afraid, and that in any case such people deserved to be pillaged'. When an officer of the National Guard politely requested him to descend, informing Caillau that he was standing on national property, he replied, with inescapable logic, that he would 'stand on the bit which belongs to me'.

Hatred of the really wealthy, fed by a very human urge to profit from the peculiar circumstances of a revolutionary situation, prompted many sans-culottes to demand a redistribution of wealth, the imposition of a maximum on the amount of money or property at the disposal of any individual. This so-called *loi agraire* so frightened the Government that it was eventually provoked into decreeing the death penalty against anyone daring to preach such perfidious doctrines. In general, however, the sans-culottes were themselves opposed to extremists. Individuals like the former priest Jacques Roux, Leclerc and Varlet, frequently referred to by historians as the *Enragés*, were bitterly attacked by 'orthodox' sans-culottes for their opposition to the Jacobins and their insistence on more positive measures against hoarders and speculators.

For the sans-culotte, social attitudes and economic theories, although important, were of less significance than political commitment. The true sans-culotte had taken part in the great revolutionary *journées*; he had fought for the democratic Republic since its inception. A man of fairly adequate means (so long as he had the decency and the good sense not to make a virtue out of his good fortune) could qualify as a sans-culotte, provided he could prove by his actions that he was prepared to risk his life for the common cause.

It was in the general assemblies and Popular Societies of the 48 Sections, into which Paris had been divided for administrative and electoral purposes in 1790, that the sans-culottes witnessed their fervour for the Revolution. Here they evolved their own brand of direct democracy—voting by acclamation, the recall of deputies who had not fulfilled their mandate, continuous correspondence between all the Sections in the pursuit of unity, fraternisation to terrorise the moderates. It was in these institutions that much of the dynamism behind the Revolution was generated—the recruitment of volunteers to fight 'the counter-revolutionary vermin in the Vendée', the collection of arms, equipment and clothing for the armies, the distribution of relief for widows and orphans. When, in the autumn of 1793, the Revolutionary Government clamped down on such meetings, the sans-culottes immediately reconstituted themselves into *sociétés sectionnaires* which, for six months, became the effective power-house of sans-culotte politics. Frequently, seized by the emotion released by a revolutionary crisis, the entire assembly of one of these societies would launch into a chorus of la Carmagnole or the Marseillaise, bestowing upon one another the fraternal kiss of friendship before closing the meeting.

The sans-culotte movement, which had been instrumental in bringing the Jacobins to power in the summer of 1793, exerted its greatest influence on the course of events during the winter of the same year. The numerical loss sustained in the conscripted and volunteer armies, the physical and emotional strain of five years of revolution, but, most of all, the incompatibility between the policies of the sans-culottes and those of the Revolutionary Government, explain the collapse of the movement by the spring of 1794. The execution of leading personalities like Hébert, Chaumette and Ronsin, the purge of the Paris Commune and the 'voluntary' disbanding of the *sociétés sectionnaires* deprived the popular movement of its élan. Emasculated by the Revolutionary Government, the sans-culottes failed to respond to the uncertain cry for help during Robespierre's own hour of crisis on 9 Thermidor. Less than one year later, the sans-culottes, provoked by the terrible famine of the Year III, were to march for the last time in the abortive spring rising of Germinal and Prairial.

The artisan and shopkeeper element were the élite, the most politically-active section, of the *classes populaires*. In the faubourg Saint-Antoine, which had an average of about a dozen or so workers to each employer, one finds a multiplicity of cabinet-makers, locksmiths, wheelwrights, sculptors in bronze and engravers. It was in this famous faubourg that we find the most positive involvement in the revolutionary cause. It should be noted, however, that the faubourg Saint-Antoine also had one of the highest percentages of *indigents*—persons qualifying for relief from the authorities—in the whole of Paris. To the north, in the Section du Faubourg-Montmartre, one finds a few hosiery and textile factories, but again this emphasis on small-scale production: there were nine carpenters employing eighty-one men; twenty-three

châtre avec sa redoutable
pique.

Charlier faisant
sa faction.

fort dela halle allant monter sa garde.

Javelier alla nt monter
sa garde.

Menuisier en faction
ze vetu de sa houpelande.

41 *Five 'sans-culottes', including a market-porter, a cobbler and a joiner,*
all armed with the 'redoubtable pike'

wheelwrights with 146 employees. 'It was indeed the craftsman who
left the strongest imprint upon the world of Parisian labour', as
Professor Soboul has noted.

This comment applies equally well to the majority of manufacturing
areas in France. In most urban centres, however, the skilled craftsman
was fighting a losing battle against the *négociant* or merchant manufacturer. Some of the bitterest battles were to be fought, not only during
the Revolution but throughout the nineteenth century, at Lyons
whose labour-force was at once more concentrated and more complex.
Almost one-third of the entire population of Lyons was engaged in
some branch or other of the silk trade. At the time of the Revolution
the city had almost 500 merchants, over 6,000 master-craftsmen who
provided work for 30,000 *compagnons* and apprentices. As in the
capital, the basic unit of production was the skilled craftsman working
with a handful of assistants. The Revolution, coming as it did after a
long period of economic stagnation, brought considerable misery and
privation to thousands of silk and textile workers, yet their political

response was never a predictable one. The ambiguous social and economic position of the craftsman, coupled with his reluctance to swallow the revolutionary cure thrust down his throat by eager Parisians, encouraged many Lyonnais to throw in their lot with the counter-revolution in the summer of 1793.

In the North-East the important textile centre of Lille provided far greater evidence of revolutionary élan, possibly because it was a frontier town. In any case, in the provinces as in Paris, only a small minority of the *classes populaires* were genuinely interested in politics: paradoxically, the 'Popular Movement' during the Revolution was the work of a very small group of activists, usually drawn from the towns. The inhabitants of the commune of Varzy in the Nièvre department were not untypical: 'wine-growers and labourers do not attend the meetings of the popular society, whilst the peasants from the surrounding countryside, who constitute about half the population of the commune, apart from one or two exceptions, are not even members of the society'.

The aspiring artisan elevated himself to the exalted rank of master-craftsman only after a lengthy, usually rigorous and often costly apprenticeship. It was customary for the *compagnon*, or journeyman, to complete the Tour de France, learning the skills of his trade in different cities and towns. *Compagnonnage* was a traditional form of working-class organisation which militated against the emergence of class-consciousness since journeymen were divided into separate groups—the *enfans de Salamon* or the *enfans de maître Jacques*—which preserved their own customs, initiation rites and signs. The journeyman had his list of addresses where he would find his *mère*, usually in an inn, who would provide him with food and shelter and put him in touch with the *rouleur* who found him employment. A rudimentary welfare service had also evolved providing sickness benefits and insurance. Napoleon favoured the growth of these early mutual-aid societies; there were over a hundred such organisations in Paris by 1812.

For those workers who possessed neither land, nor trade nor any particular skill, life tended to be 'nasty, brutish and short'. In the big textile centres, spinners and weavers were usually among the most deprived section of the community, forced to harness the energy of their children from the tenderest ages in order to make a living. In

Lyons, workers 'from the cradle to the grave learn nothing but how to handle silk and then how to make cloth, possessing neither the strength nor the skill for any other profession'. A Napoleonic journal, the *Décade philosophique*, describing the condition of the working classes in Lyons, found them 'in a truly miserable condition, drawn and emaciated, crowded into their tiny rooms alongside their wives, children, sick relatives and their looms'. A report by the Prefect of Paris, dated May 1807, underlines the poor physical condition of many workers in the capital: bakers' assistants, 'who at 50 are practically senile, usually suffering from catarrh and asthma'; shoemakers, prone to pulmonary diseases, 'an old shoemaker is a rare sight'; textile workers, 'who are really nothing but machines themselves'. One piece of social legislation was passed in January 1813—children under ten years of age were no longer to be employed in the mines!

Just as there were relatively few factories so there was nothing comparable to the modern department-store. The purchase of anything from a gold necklace to a handkerchief was a very personal affair, the bargain not uncommonly struck in the street itself. In the cities and towns, street-stalls and street-vendors supplied most of the more mundane articles of food and clothing. There were of course the big markets, such as the relatively new Wheat Market in Paris which supplied grain wholesale on Wednesdays and Saturdays, or the Fish Market which, lacking refrigeration, could usually be found by following one's own nose. The retail trade, however, was a very intimate one: the corner-street grocer, the confectioner, the wine-merchant, the butcher, the baker and the candle-stick maker all knew their clientele personally. This close relationship of both craftsman and shopkeeper with their customers was one of the distinguishing features of eighteenth-century urban society; it helps to explain the involvement of these groups in the events of the Revolution. Bakers, possibly the most unenviable professional group in the Revolution, were subjected to strict surveillance both by the police and the public. The faubourg Saint-Antoine alone had over 100 bakers: there were six times this number in Paris as a whole.

The problem of supplying Paris and the larger provincial towns with food and other essential commodities was undertaken by an army of transport workers—bargees, carters, heavers, lock-keepers, market-

42   *Madame Montansier's theatre in the Palais-Royal was one of the many 'dens of iniquity' denounced by the sans-culottes*

porters who kept goods flowing along the main arteries of eighteenth-century France, the canals, roads and rivers. These workers were regarded by the police with considerable suspicion, if not fear, since most food-riots occurred in the ports, docks, canals or small-town markets. As Richard Cobb has remarked, the police in eighteenth-century France were convinced that 'trouble walked on the water'. Physically robust, usually on the move, such workers presented a problem to the police as purveyors of gossip as well as of groceries.

One of the most striking features of French society at this time was the mobility of its population, at least so far as urban society and particularly the capital was concerned. The Revolution posed new problems for a harassed police-force constantly striving, against tremendous odds, to keep some kind of check on new arrivals in the cities. Every autumn Paris welcomed its annual quota of seasonal workers—wood-floaters from the Yonne, a particularly brutal and, to the police, unwelcome addition to the indigenous population; masons and building-labourers from the Limousin; water-carriers (Paris had several thousand) from the Auvergne, 'whose bodies, bent in order to balance the load on their shoulders, could hardly be adapted to any other job'; chimney-sweeps and odd-job men from Savoy, the former using children of seven or eight with bandaged eyes and heads covered with a sack to do the initial cleaning; dealers in second-hand goods and porters, 'who carried loads on their backs heavy enough to kill a horse'. Some of these seasonal workers eventually made their homes permanently in Paris or Marseille, swelling the ranks of an urban population which had its feet firmly planted in the provinces.

According to many contemporary reports, prostitution posed a major problem, if not to the police, then certainly to the custodians of public morality. Estimates of 25,000-30,000 prostitutes in Paris, although difficult to confirm, could not have been very wide of the mark. The visitor to the capital at the beginning of the Revolution could easily obtain on the boulevards a little booklet informing him of the addresses, the prices and the service he could obtain. During the Terror, the sans-culotte authorities tried to eradicate this blot on the reputation of the infant Republic, but with little success. Attempts to establish 'parthenons' where ladies of easy virtue might be rehabilitated in accordance with classical and republican precepts bordered on the comical. Prostitutes continued to lurk behind the pillars of the Palais Royal, eventually moving onto the aggressive under the Directory. As with most régimes, prostitution in the bigger cities was closely associated with crime and provided a valuable source of information for the police.

Throughout our period it was the problem of bread which exercised the minds of governments and the stomachs of the *classes populaires*. The purchase of bread alone consumed over half the daily wage of an unskilled or semi-skilled worker—a percentage which was far higher in times of crisis. Unlike many of his provincial counterparts the Parisian worker was almost as concerned with the quality as with the quantity of his bread: Government officials visiting the Wheat Market in the crisis month of April 1795 were subjected to a torrent of abuse from irate and hungry women protesting that the small amount of rationed bread provided was only fit for pigs. In September 1793, the Jacobin government, appreciating the close relationship between bread and the barricades, agreed somewhat reluctantly to place a ceiling on the cost of basic food-supplies. For over a year the *classes populaires* enjoyed their *pain de l'égalité* supplied according to the provisions of the General Maximum, but with the fall of the Jacobins in the summer of 1794 the Maximum, together with the machinery of repression which ensured its enforcement, was gradually dismantled, provoking the appalling misery and hardship of the winter and spring of the Year III. The Revolution, so far as material well-being is concerned, had brought little joy: the final years of the eighteenth century were among the most miserable in the long collective memory of 'le peuple'. For many the only alternative to starvation was to join the swollen ranks of beggars, brigands or the slightly more respectable battalions of the Republican Armies.

Years of dearth like 1795-6 or 1812 were invariably followed by massive epidemics of dysentery, cholera or typhus, and, as one might expect, it was the poorer classes, huddled together in the overcrowded and unsanitary *quartiers* of the cities, who suffered most. Paris, for all its colour and variety—the dress, dialects and accents of provincials and foreigners, 'the small shrill, impatient voice of the marquis mingling with the frightful curses of carters, the shouts of water-carriers, scrap-merchants and fishwives'—was not altogether a pleasant city in which to live. Refuse collection was rudimentary; there were many open sewers and butchers often slaughtered animals on the premises, leaving the blood and unwanted carcasses to disappear 'by natural causes' on the streets. There were very few pavements, and measures to protect health, prevent fires or provide an adequate lighting system were woefully inadequate. For a couple of sous one could make use of the planks carried by Savoyards to facilitate the crossing of muddy rivulets after heavy rainfall; or, after a visit to the theatre, hire a *falot*, a man carrying a lantern, which not only provided light for pedestrians but also offered some protection against robbery.

Yet, when one has tabulated the misery provoked by a fairly heartless society, produced graphs to show the high incidence of suicide in 1796 or deaths from cholera and typhus during the last years of the Empire, one is still confronted with a residual enjoyment of life amongst the *classes populaires* which appears, at first glance, inexplicable. There were times, however, when 'joy was unconfined'; for example, the Sunday visits to the small, crowded inns on the outskirts of Paris, the traditional inns and *cabarets* of Courtille and Ivry which offered enough

43   *An afternoon or evening spent in a little inn (guinguette) on the outskirts of Paris promised pleasure for the entire family*

cheap wine and spirits to make even the poorest Parisian forget his hunger. Drunkenness was common; it was a brave bourgeois who dared to confront a worker returning to his furnished room on a Sunday or Monday evening—the police rarely made an appearance.

One could also borrow a cart or hire a carriage to attend the various *fêtes champêtres* organised during the summer in the little villages around Paris, Saint Maur, Vincennes or Choissy. There were many *bals populaires* and the boulevards of the bigger cities provided a variety of entertainment from 'the invisible women in the glass case' or 'the incombustible Spaniard' to all kinds of fortune-telling, lotteries, popular, usually crude, farces and melodramas produced in the tiny boulevard theatres. Rétif de la Bretonne describes how apprentices and warehousemen passed their leisure hours in billiard-halls and gaming-houses where the innocent visitor was easily 'fleeced' by a horde of professional tricksters. During the Empire there were of course the military parades. Napoleon believed implicitly in the virtues of 'bread and circuses' for keeping the masses in line, such as the Imperial bun-feast held on 3 December 1804 when meat, wine and bread were distributed to the lower orders to the traditional accompaniment of fireworks and dancing.

For the artisan who was reasonably successful at his craft there was the occasional outing for the family to one of the better theatres or even a restaurant. Very few could afford to eat too often in the fashionable

44   *Fortune-telling was as popular in the eighteenth century as it is today*

restaurants of the Palais Royal, if indeed at all, but there were establishments which catered for those with limited incomes. During the Empire, apart from the crisis years after 1812, food was relatively plentiful and cheap. The discerning housewife could get a pound of stewing-beef for around fifteen sous, a pound of butter for one franc eight sous, a chicken for about two francs and a bottle of claret for less than fifteen sous.

Such price-lists, however, are fairly meaningless unless they are related in some way to earnings. The majority of small-scale craftsmen earned between two and three francs a day; printers and engravers were worth a little more whilst the really skilled goldsmith, jeweller or ebonist earned a minimum of six to seven francs a day. When one considers that a family of four had to pay well over a franc a day for bread alone one can appreciate that there was little left over for the luxuries of life. Of course, some wives worked as laundresses or in the markets, a few even as water-carriers or street-vendors, and there were the children who could be relied upon to supplement the family income. However, women rarely earned over one franc a day, whilst in Réveillon's wall-paper factory in Paris children came home with the princely sum of twelve sous for a fourteen-hour day. In towns like Orleans, where over 2,000 workers were engaged in the cap and hosiery industry, and Nîmes, where many more were employed in silk and cloth manufacture, wages tended to be artificially depressed owing to the importance of domestic industry in the surrounding countryside. With the decline of the guilds and the anti-working class legislation passed during the Revolution, such as the Loi Chapelier of 1791, the scope for organised protest was limited, although tailors, hatters and printers were quite prominent in strike activities during this period.

The result was that the less affluent of the *classes populaires* spent their incomes on the four basic commodities which ensured survival— bread, wine, wood for heating and perhaps a little meat. If the housewife could not afford the butcher's prices there was always the *regratteur* who sold pieces of meat bought or stolen from hotels, restaurants or private homes. Mercier stated that three-quarters of the inhabitants of Paris lived off bread, thin soup, with perhaps a little meat in the evenings or on Sundays. Vegetables were regarded as something of a luxury. Elsewhere, as at Lyons, dried fish might form part of the staple

45 *Gracchus Babeuf, represented here as the evil figure about to plunge its dagger into the fair personification of bourgeois France, led an abortive plot in 1796. He has been regarded, mainly by Marxist historians as the forerunner of Blanqui and Lenin*

diet, or, as in the South-East, fruit and even chestnuts. From the limited statistical evidence available it appears that the *classes populaires* were marginally better fed during the Revolution and Empire than during the first half of the nineteenth century.

The Revolution enabled the *classes populaires,* for a brief period, to politicise their grievances; only a small minority availed themselves of the opportunity and these brave few suffered for their insolence after the fall of Robespierre. It is true that one man, Gracchus Babeuf, a former *feudiste* from Picardy, did organise in 1796 the 'Conspiracy of the Equals' which modern Marxist historians consider to have been the first truly working-class movement, but so far as the vast majority of workers were concerned Babeuf's ideas were further removed from the reality of their daily lives than the Monarchy had been before 1789. For at least the Monarchy had taken a paternalistic interest in the welfare of the people (more out of fear than love it is true) and some aristocrats had not lived exclusively for the profit-motive. The future promised little for the *classes populaires* other than the gradual disappearance of their traditional skills, customs and pastimes, although, in many ways, the cult of the craftsman and the small shopkeeper has proved to be an enduring feature of the social and economic history of France.

6 Popular Violence and Government Repression

Common to most agrarian and largely illiterate communities violence was woven into the fabric of eighteenth-century French society: it was to condition the response of many to the Revolution. In Paris, good, respectable citizens were imprisoned after the downfall of the Jacobins as *buveurs de sang*; the crimes and atrocities committed by both sides during the great Vendean uprising fell far short of the human values proclaimed by many revolutionaries; the South had its own vocabulary of violence. Whenever central authority was weak, as in the autumn of 1793 or again from 1795 to 1799, the latent violence of the countryside erupted in the form of pillage, assassination and brigandage, continuing the pattern of eighteenth century social upheavals, although obviously assuming a more political guise during the Revolution. The exploits of 'Jourdan, the head-chopper' in Avignon, or 'Trestaillons, the butcher' in Nîmes were paralleled by those of the legendary brigands of the mid-eighteenth century, such as Mandrin in the Dauphiné. The pressures of war and revolution occasionally produced frenzied outbursts of collective and retributive justice; the individual merged into the revolutionary crowd assumes a very different identity: 'What person does not go a little beyond himself in a revolution?' asked one prisoner arrested in 1794 for his terrorist activities during the previous year.

Ancien régime France had spread its veneer of culture over the surface of western European society: it had made precious little impact upon the mass of the people. It is 'a picture of a brutal, violent and primitive society', which contemporary observers such as Louis Sébastien Mercier and Rétif de la Bretonne paint for us. The Bourbons had treated the people with a mixture of fear and contempt, occasionally tolerating their periodic bouts of violence, prepared to bargain, to temporise, but when all else failed, subjecting them to brutal repression. Branding, torture, the galleys, breaking on the wheel, the whole grisly ceremony of public executions formed as integral a part of French

46 *'Jourdan, the Head-chopper'* conducted a personal reign of terror in and around Avignon at the beginning of the Revolution

life as religious processions and village fêtes. Invariably well-attended, public executions were supposed to teach the putative criminal that crime did not pay; in fact they did little more than pander to the more sadistic and voyeuristic tendencies of the human condition.

As the population expanded fairly rapidly so social problems became more acute. On the eve of the Revolution, over 6,000 children were abandoned in Paris, twice as many as in 1770. One of the largest hospitals in the capital, the Hôtel-Dieu, had 5,000 patients, but only 1,200 beds, 'in which the sick were laid side by side with the dying, thrown into an atmosphere polluted by every kind of disease'. At dawn each morning, carts would leave the hospitals filled with corpses destined for the cemeteries at Clamart where they would be thrown into lime-pits. Crimes against property increased in the course of the century, giving rise to a battery of new laws designed to protect the property-owner. In both town and countryside the problems of begging and brigandage became more acute.

To deal with this increased volume of crime and violence the *ancien régime* had only the skeleton of a police force. It is true that Paris was relatively well-served: the Lieutenant de police had 1,500 men under his direct control, plus several hundred more in reserve, but their duties included not only routine police matters but the supervision of food-supplies, fire-fighting, the prevention of floods, even the provision of wet-nurses for Parisian families. During a crisis, the Lieutenant was obliged to fall back upon the Gardes françaises, whose social composition and sympathies were not that far removed from the people they were called upon to keep in order, and who were not always above using crime, particularly prostitution, for their own purposes. Throughout France the forces of repression were woefully inadequate, which explains why so many local authorities were obliged to compromise when faced with a full-scale riot—time had to be bought in order to allow regular troops to be brought into the troubled area from distant garrisons. In some ways, however, things were easier for the police than in our own day. In eighteenth-century society a bourgeois dressed like a bourgeois; a worker was generally attired in the costume of his trade, complete with a metal plaque denoting his profession and his number.

The 'problem of the cities' and the demand for 'law and order' provoked as much debate in the 1780s as it has done in more recent times. A major issue on the eve of the Revolution, it became a far greater problem a decade later. The Revolution made the task of the already harassed *commissaire de police* far more difficult. He could still consult his police manual, of course, which told him that peddlers, dealers in second-hand goods, porters, laundresses and sailors were generally to be regarded with suspicion, and that anyone from Lyons or Nîmes started life in the capital at a distinct disadvantage, but with the introduction of a whole new category of political crimes and criminals, the old guide-lines tended to be inadequate. The Napoleonic Empire, with the experience of the Revolution to fall back upon, was to introduce new methods of repression, although, by the creation of massive armies and the copious spilling of French and foreign blood on the battlefields, Napoleon successfully released many of the internal social pressures which had not been unrelated to the violence of the pre-revolutionary and revolutionary era.

Much of the drama of the Revolution was to be enacted on the streets. The memorable *journées*—14 July and 5 October 1789; 10 August 1792; 2 June and 5 September 1793 and the final abortive uprisings

47   *The heads of two government officials being paraded on pikes*
during the journée *of 14 July 1789*

of 1795—mark successive stages in the march of the Revolution when
the 'common people', through violence, helped to resolve the deadlock
between the Court and the Third Estate, or, as in 1793, between rival
factions within the National Assembly. The rise of the Jacobins to
power, and the form which the Terror eventually assumed in 1793,
were directly associated with the pressure of *le peuple*. The course, as
much as the character, of the Revolution was noticeably affected by the
tradition of the barricades which can be traced back at least to the
Fronde uprisings of the mid-seventeenth century. This tradition was
to be repeatedly invoked during the nineteenth century and, with less
success, in our own day.

Those who participated in the *journées* were not the zoological
specimens delineated by historians such as Taine, 'the creatures of the
forests', or 'the rats of the sewers'; they were, according to the detailed

48　*The Palais-Royal was the Hyde Park of revolutionary Paris*

analyses of Professor Rudé, mainly drawn from the workshop- and shop-keeper-element of Parisian society, relatively young and provincial in origin. Such an analysis is particularly relevant to the more political *journées* such as 10 August 1792 or 2 June 1793. In the Réveillon riots of April 1789 and the demonstration at the Champs de Mars in 1791, day-labourers and the unemployed played a more significant, although still minor role. Women played a very important part in provoking food-riots in October 1789 and again in the spring of 1795. It is probable

—although only an unproven hypothesis—that the *classes dangereuses*
contributed more to these *journées* than recent historical studies
suggest.

Apart from the exception of August and September 1792, the
journées were not characterised by excessive or blind vengeance on
the part of the crowd. In the Réveillon riots, the hundreds of dead and
wounded which lay in the streets were demonstrators not soldiers;
only a handful of those defending the Bastille lost their lives on 14 July,
whereas 150 insurgents were killed. Again, during the Champs de Mars

49   *Troops were used by the government only as a last resort,*
but with bloody consequences

affair in 1791 it was the demonstrators, numbering about fifty, who paid
with their lives. No one was killed, however, during the *journée* of
31 May—2 June 1793. Indeed it can be said that indiscriminate slaughter
was the exception rather than the rule, the exception being the summer
months of August and September 1792 when, owing to the obstruction
of the Court and the pressure of foreign invasion, Paris witnessed
scenes of violence unparalleled in what was a fairly violent century.
During the storming of the Tuileries on 10 August, having lost over
300 of their own men, the insurgents slaughtered over 600 royal troops.
In the worst paroxysm of collective, although not altogether spontane-
ous violence, well over 1,000 prisoners, the majority guilty of no
political crimes, were butchered during the September Massacres in
peculiarly distressing circumstances. Acts of extreme cruelty were
committed, but for men accustomed to seeing criminals hung, drawn
and quartered or broken on the wheel a delicate approach to killing was
hardly to be expected.

To break down the composition of the crowd into its respective social categories tells us little about why people acted as they did. Irrational, psychological, even biological factors must be taken into account. In the summer of 1792 the crowd was spurred to action by fear of the advancing Prussian armies, fear of a 'prison plot' to massacre women and children whilst the sans-culottes were busily repulsing the enemy at Longwy and Valmy. The exigencies of a revolutionary situation, aggravated by a serious military crisis, laid bare the raw nerve of action. The same emotional pressures which, in times of victory, led members of a Popular Society to break out spontaneously into the Marseillaise produced, in a more desperate hour, acts of collective and punitive violence which lost the sans-culottes the sympathy of English intellectuals like Wordsworth or Coleridge, who thought that revolutions could be exorcised through poetry rather than the pike.

50 *Crowds besiege the Opera House in Paris : art was to be 'purified' and 'politicised' by the sans-culottes*

51 *Women played an important role in the genesis of insurrectionary situations*

Despite its pre-eminent role in the Revolution, Paris did not possess by any means a monopoly of violence: in any geography of death the South-East must take pride of place. Over 300 Catholic Royalists were massacred by Protestant Republicans in Nîmes in 1790; Jourdan and 'ses braves brigands du Vaucluse', accounted for scores of victims in and around Avignon; during the White Terror of 1795, royalist gangs committed their depredations and assassinations throughout the South with impunity, including prison massacres on the Parisian pattern. Nothing in Paris equalled the ferocity of the Vendean uprisings in which thousands of peasants, artisans and Government troops lost their lives. Such counter-revolutionary movements must be regarded as 'popular movements', since, for the local populations involved, the struggle against the incursion of urban values into a profoundly rural and provincial society was a popular one. Much of the history of the Revolution can be written in terms of traditional antagonisms between Paris and the provinces, between town and countryside.

During the summer of 1793, especially after the expulsion of the Girondins from the Assembly, the Government began to re-establish control over a country torn by internal dissension and war. The

Constituent Assembly had decentralised France, facilitating the growth of local counter-revolutionary resistance. By the Law of Frimaire Year II (4 December 1793) the Jacobins reimposed a form of centralisation: the departments were replaced as administrative units by the districts; the post of *agent national* was created to link the provinces with the central Government. Given the problems of a wartime crisis, and the persistant pressure of the sans-culotterie for more organised terror allied to Robespierre's exclusive definition of civic duty, which branded all those who were not *for* the Revolution as potential traitors, the work of the Revolutionary Government of the Year II, however noble in design, became increasingly harsh and repressive in execution. Well over 30,000 individuals had fallen to the 'scythe of equality' before the Robespierrists sealed one of the bloodiest chapters in the Revolution with their own deaths in July 1794. Thirty thousand deaths might appear a rather trifling figure when compared with the holocausts of the twentieth century; it does illustrate, however, that, whether before or during the Revolution, the violence of the crowd was completely overshadowed by the repressive action of governments.

During the Terror, from the summer of 1793 to that of 1794, there was only one *journée*, the demonstration of 5 September 1793. Compared with its predecessors, it was little more than a peaceful show of strength. Retribution could now safely be left to the Jacobins who took such things seriously, far too seriously at times. The infamous Law of Suspects of 17 September 1793 which laid down the broadest possible definition of treachery, was passed, in part, to forestall any recurrence of the September Massacres of 1792. Again, as a result of popular pressure, the Revolutionary Tribunal, the legal arm of the Committee of General Security, which had first been created in March 1793, was purged and its powers considerably increased. With the great Committee of Public Safety deciding major internal and external policy, police affairs were left almost entirely to the Committee of General Security. Through its national network of Popular Societies and *comités de surveillance*, its army of informers and spies strategically placed in practically every political meeting, port and prison in France, the Committee of General Security provided the Jacobin government with the most efficient police-service in the history of France.

The acceleration of the Terror is accurately reflected in the activities

52 *An exaggerated but not totally inaccurate depiction of 'popular justice' during the September massacres*

of the Revolutionary Tribunal, its work expedited by that soulless type of Public Prosecutor beloved of every police régime, Fouquier-Tinville. Less than thirty prisoners were condemned to death by the Tribunal in August and September 1793; six times this number went to the guillotine in the following three months, including the Queen, the duc d'Orleans and leading Girondists. Fouquier-Tinville began to develop the technique of throwing prisoners together in 'batches'—if there were not enough Queens or dukes to go round, one could always find a foreign agent, a banker or a refractory priest to prejudice in the popular mind the fate of the innocent as all stood together in the dock.

The effectiveness of the Terror is also reflected in the marked increase in the prison population of Paris and the bigger provincial cities. Fear of a 'prison plot' had helped to provoke the September Massacres; the same fear continued to excite the imagination of patriots throughout the Terror. The reason is not difficult to discover. Prisons during the Revolution were notoriously easy places from which to escape. Due to overcrowding, new and makeshift institutions had to be opened such as the Luxembourg, the Port-Libre and Les Carmes in Paris and since they were not originally designed as prisons it is hardly surprising that they failed to meet the requirements of such institutions. Visiting was also extremely liberal, particularly if the warder was paid for his assistance; it was by no means unknown for prisoners to bring their beds or even rent a better cell; not all cells had iron bars; relatively few had doors and there was usually no curfew. The wife of the gaoler of La Madelonnettes treated her inmates as 'boarders', and provided one had the money or the influence life in prison could be tolerable; André Chénier continued to write his poetry, whilst the great actor Larive organised plays in the Port-Libre. The vision, constantly invoked by the sans-culottes, of infernal plots being concocted over sumptuous dinners, was not altogether without foundation.

However informal the atmosphere (and a perceptible change occurred during the autumn of 1793) the increase of the Terror made life far more unbearable. There was always the danger of *les moutons*—the prison informers of the Committee of General Security—and, hanging like a sword of Damocles above one's head, the dreaded moment when one's name was read out as one of those to be executed the following day. For the poor, who could not afford what little luxuries were available through bribery, there were only stinking, straw mattresses, insufficient food, and perhaps seven or eight people crammed into one cell with the

53   *Awaiting the roll-call for 'madame guillotine'. The figure seated in the centre of the picture is the poet Chénier*

54   *Inside the St Lazare prison*

ever-present threat of disease. In the more feared prisons, such as the
Abbaye or the Conciergerie, conditions by the beginning of 1794 were
quite appalling.

The Terror, although necessarily more fitful and sporadic in its
impact, exacted a far greater toll in the provinces than in Paris. During
the autumn and winter of 1793 the Government dispatched Representatives-on-Mission to propagate the gospel of the Revolution to a largely
apathetic, occasionally downright hostile, population. Armed with
powers of life and death, often, like Javoques in the Loire, paying only
lip-service to the directives of the central Government, many of these
Representatives were primarily responsible for exacting a terrible
vengeance in the provinces. Vidocq, a thief, army deserter, and like
so many of his kind, one of Napoleon's police officers, recalled as a

young man in Arras watching Representative Lebon, resplendent in his black uniform, tricolour sashes, republican hat and a brace of pistols tucked into his belt, presiding over the execution of an elderly man whilst an orchestra interspersed with deafening fanfares each sentence of the official proclamation of death.

Only the dress and the revolutionary rhetoric distinguished such occasions from the public executions of the *ancien régime*; this was not something entirely new, simply different. What was new was the scale of this repression in places like Lyons and Nantes. In the former city Fouché (who surpassed Vidocq by becoming Napoleon's Minister of Police) and Collot d'Herbois organised the execution of hundreds of victims by lining them up before open graves, then dispatching them with cannon-fire. In Nantes, Carrier devised an even quicker and less harrowing procedure by drowning over 2,000 prisoners, many of them priests, in the river Loire.

In some places, for example at Lyons, the Representatives-on-Mission were assisted by detachments of the Parisian Revolutionary Army. Specialists in terror, having served their apprenticeship in the Sections of Paris, it was to these experts that local militants appealed for guidance. If the Parisian Revolutionary Army did not actually carry out the grisly task of massacre, it certainly proved invaluable in arresting suspects in Lyons. The political activities of the Revolutionary Armies were no doubt of less significance than their work in ensuring the flow of essential food-supplies; they were nonetheless important in bringing certain areas to a state bordering upon anarchy during the winter of 1793.

In addition to the Parisian detachments, many departmental armies, not all of them legally constituted, further weakened the authority of the elected administrative organs of government. In parts of Brittany, the South-West, the Massif Central and Alsace, 'Revolutionary Armies reigned supreme, behaving as if they controlled a conquered country, dismissing officials, arresting or freeing individuals . . . sweeping away duly elected bodies and legal objections.' They were often encouraged by *représentants* like Taillefer in the Aveyron—'no quarter for these swine'—or Carrier in the Loire who, according to one of the most notorious leaders of a departmental army, Le Batteux, ordered him 'to shoot down aristocrats, nobles and fanatical priests'.

Shocking as the worst atrocities of the Terror were, they must be placed in their geographical and historical context. It was precisely in and around those areas where resistance to the Revolution had been most pronounced, and where revolutionaries themselves had suffered most acutely, that the most terrible acts of repression occurred. Over seventy per cent of the total number of executions recorded in France during the Terror took place in the West and the South-East, and even here repression was confined to relatively limited areas—if Nantes mourned its dead in hundreds, the neighbouring city of Rouen lost barely a dozen citizens. It is also evident that the authority of both Representatives-on-Mission and the various Revolutionary Armies was limited in time and space. The great majority of the communes of France, particularly if they were off the main trade or communication routes, survived the Terror, and indeed the Revolution, unmolested; or if they were honoured by a visit from a Javoques or a Fréron, accompanied perhaps by a detachment of the Revolutionary Army, the villagers did their best to match for a day the verbal extravagances of hardened revolutionaries, only to return to their daily tasks as the last cloud of dust filtered away behind the retreating republican columns.

Having cleaned up the main pockets of counter-revolution and satisfied at least a few of the demands of the sans-culotterie, the Robespierrists applied themselves to the more positive, albeit rather hopeless, task of creating their Republic of Virtue. The essence of Robespierre's boring and somewhat menacing belief in *vertu* and the need for unity is to be found in a speech made, inappropriately enough, on Christmas Day 1793: '*Vertu* is simple, modest, humble, often ignorant, sometimes boorish; it is the natural lot of the poor, the patrimony of the people. Vice is surrounded by wealth, armed with every desire to lure the voluptuary and ensnare the weak . . . How swiftly the seeds of division which (tyrants) sow among us may grow unless we choke them from the start.' The philosophy of the eighteenth century with its naive confidence in human progress and the perfectibility of Man through precept and instruction is implicit in much of Robespierre's writings. The millennium could be achieved, but first it was necessary to kill dissension at the root. If this also meant getting rid of a few popular, personal enemies, so much the better.

The Representatives-on-Mission were recalled; the departmental

55 *Maximilien Robespierre, dubbed the 'Incorruptible'*

MAXIMILIEN MARIE ISIDORE.
ROBESPIERRE
Députe' de la Province d'Artois,
Du superbe oppresseur ennemi redoutable,
Incorruptible ami du peuple qu'on accable;
Il fait briller au sein des viles factions,
Les vertus d'Aristide etl'âme des Catons.

and ultimately the Parisian Revolutionary Armies were disbanded; a halt was called to the programme of dechristianisation and the bloodier aspects of the Terror in the provinces. But such moves did not eliminate factional and personal disputes. The antagonisms of the early months of 1794 developed into a debate over which faction should control the potential violence of a revolutionary situation. The popular demagogue Hébert and his sympathisers called for more bloodshed, a tightening-up of the Terror: Danton, Desmoulins and their followers sought an end to the purges and the blood-letting. At the end of March and the beginning of April 1794, the Revolutionary Government decided, in Robespierre's phraseology, to 'choke both factions from the start'. On 24 March, Hébert and seventeen others were sent to the guillotine, to be followed less than a fortnight later by the Dantonists.

The inexorable logic of Jacobin repression in the pursuit of that elusive quality, *vertu*, increased the severity of the Terror in Paris over the next few months. Two separate attempts on Robespierre's life provided some excuse for the Law of Prairial which expedited the work of the Revolutionary Tribunal by denying the basic rights of defence to the accused. Between March 1793 and the first week of June 1794, 1,251 people had been executed; during the next two months 1,376 victims climbed the steps of the guillotine. Eighty-four per cent of the total number of persons executed during the Terror came from the ranks of the Third Estate, thus providing a very different picture from that delineated in fiction by a d'Orczy or a Dickens.

Unfortunately for the Jacobins, this increase in the Terror coincided with a relaxation of the wartime crisis. On 26 June, the French won the battle of Fleurus against the Austrians which opened up the road to Brussels and the occupation of Belgium. Little wonder that people were frightened, bewildered and indeed sickened by the mounting scale of bloodshed, all in the pursuit of some far distant millennium: 'The rumbling of the carts filled with victims instilled a sense of fear and horror, bringing trade to a virtual standstill in the richest parts of Paris. As soon as the time approached for this grisly parade, shops closed their doors, people shuttered their windows and took refuge in the back-rooms of their apartments.' The Government recognised the general revulsion by moving the scene of these executions from the Place de la Révolution to the more distant Barrière du Trône.

The Revolutionary Government had begun its work with an idealistic vision of a regenerated France. The authoritarian aspects of its policies were but temporary expedients, due partly to the requirements of a wartime crisis, to ensure the eradication of evil and the subsequent promotion of the reign of justice and humanity: the ends justified the means. Eventually however the means triumphed over the ends. In a revealing comment made by one contemporary a few weeks after the fall of the Robespierrists it was noted that, 'the members of the Committee of General Security came to resemble the old lieutenants de police, and those of the Committee of Public Safety the former Ministers of State'. The burden of office had imposed its own logic.

One of the worst legacies of the Terror was the 'license to kill' which it gave to various groups and individuals. For the next five years, but

56   *Brigandage was endemic in many parts of France, particularly between 1795 and 1800*

particularly in 1795, revenge, personal vendettas and feuds took precedence over political issues. The apathy and cynicism which the last months of the Terror had bred, the dismantling of the machinery of repression, the abandonment of any attempt to coerce the French into any doctrinaire mould, led to a period in which the credibility gap between the slogans of a revolution and the reality of everyday life became increasingly wide. In the void thus created, the more traditional forms of violence, unchecked in many parts of France by any sign of strong government, were once again unleashed.

In the Nord, the Var, Rousillon and Normandy, landless peasants, blacksmiths, wheelwrights, horse-dealers, peddlers and army deserters, leavened occasionally with a sprinkling of petty nobles and non-juring priests, formed terrorist bands whose depredations continued well into the reign of Napoleon. In the department of the Gard, the first prefect installed complained that his most difficult problem in restoring 'law and order' involved *les fanatiques*, gangs of Catholic Royalist bandits, who controlled the hills to the north of the department. In the department of the Seine-Inférieure, the activities of Duramé and his companions terrorised the area for several years; whilst in the Rhenish provinces which had been overrun by the French, the name of Schinderhannes aroused fear in the hearts of lonely cottagers and farmers. The character of brigandage underwent an important transformation as a result of the Revolution, becoming more disciplined (the influence of so many army deserters), more secretive and far more permanent. There is also little doubt that in the North and the South-East more brutal methods were employed in the pursuit of pillage and plunder. Occasionally, it is very difficult to make a distinction between traditional brigandage and counter-revolutionary movements, yet another consequence of the Revolution.

The year 1795 marked the peak of the 'White Terror' in the South with the reappearance of royalist gangs (see also page 126). Given the ferocity of the repression in Lyons during the Terror it is not surprising that the survivors or the relatives of the hundreds of victims of the Jacobin period should have exacted a terrible revenge. Armed bands describing themselves as the *Compagnie de Jésus* or the *Compagnie de Jéhu* roamed the area paying off old debts, massacring prisoners. Over a hundred people lost their lives in Lyons; three times this number in the entire department. In the months of May and June 1795, over fifty people were assassinated in Aix, forty-seven in Tarascon. Avignon continued to witness those scenes of violence to which it had become accustomed since 1789. 'Sur le pont d'Avignon' people not only danced but periodically disposed of bodies into the accommodating river Rhône. In Nîmes, the mayor during the Terror, Courbis, was one of the victims of a band of assassins who broke into the prison killing and mutilating several former terrorists. Anyone who had held office during the Terror slept uneasily in his bed during the summer of 1795: during the Revolution an official's lot was not a particularly happy one.

The rise to power of Napoleon saw the introduction of new and more efficient administrative and repressive institutions. Troops successfully dealt with the chronic problem of brigandage; the institution of the prefectorial system effectively centralised the administration: gradually, every aspect of public life—religion, the press, labour movements and political activities—was closely supervised and controlled. The Civil and Criminal Codes rationalized and expedited judicial procedures, although with the reintroduction of arbitrary arrests, the secrecy of court proceedings in certain instances and the

57 *With the creation of the prefectoral system Napoleon completed the work of the Bourbon Kings in centralising France*

creation of Exceptional Tribunals, something more than a faint whiff of *ancien régime* practice could be detected.

The Ministry of Police was made far more efficient. Under the direction of its notorious head, the ex-terrorist Fouché, the methods of the Committee of General Security were refined and brought under the immediate control of a man with a peculiar genius for prying into every aspect of public and personal life. With an ex-terrorist at the top and an ex-convict, Vidocq, creating a department under the Prefect of Police which was to prove the forerunner of the present-day Sûreté, Paris became one of the best policed cities in Europe. On the principle that it was better to 'set a thief to catch a thief', Vidocq generally employed ex-convicts who were paid on a commission basis according to the number of arrests they made. Paris was divided into districts, and, although there was no clearly-defined central organization, a start had been made in the creation of a modern apparatus of criminal detection.

With the failure of the Popular Movement during the Revolution political attacks under the Empire became far more élitist and secretive, a transformation which began with Babeuf and the Conspiracy of the Equals. The Cadoudal plot of 1804—launched with the connivance of the British government—was no more successful than Babeuf's, ending in one of the very few 'mass executions' of the Napoleonic period when twelve conspirators were guillotined in the Place de Grève. Such public executions evoked memories of the Reign of Terror, although, during the Empire, they proved to be the exception rather than the rule. There were a number of executions for rioting after the crisis year of 1812, but the Government, although repressive, was never obliged to resort to the methods of 1793. The attention of Frenchmen, most of whom were not sorry to forget the bloodier aspects of the Revolution, was further diverted from internecine struggles by Napoleon's military victories and the seemingly endless search for *la gloire*. Napoleon's victory over internal disorder was partly won on the foreign battle-fields of Marengo, Jéna and Austerlitz.

If political movements declined during the Empire, at least until after 1812, the period proved to be a relatively fertile one for the common criminal, the army deserter and the smuggler. Most governments get the criminals they deserve; the trinity of outlaws listed above was almost automatically produced by a society which put its emphasis on the acquisition of wealth, and by a Government which appeared to rest at times solely upon the recruiting-sergeant and the customs-official. The Empire produced some notable, almost legendary criminals like Barthélemy Lacour, nick-named Coco, 'educated by prostitutes and trained by apprenticed thieves' (needless to say, Coco eventually joined the ranks of the police), Desnoyers, 'the master of disguise', and Desfossieux, 'the Houdini of the Empire'. Vidocq, having lived amongst them, knew his clientele, the pickpockets, the house-breakers, the highwaymen; he knew that the best day for a crime was a Sunday, rising to a new peak at the end of the quarter when people often moved themselves (and other people's possessions) from one set of furnished rooms to another in order to avoid paying the rent. Through his wife, Annette, who kept a tavern in the rue de l'Orme, he kept in touch with the underworld of crime.

The violence and bloodshed associated with this period was the product of war as much as of a revolutionary situation, of traditional social and economic forces which during the Revolution assumed a more political form. The Law of Suspects of 1793 simply gave the *commiss-aires de police* far wider power of arrest to imprison much the same categories of people—the *gens sans aveu*, the itinerant worker, as well as the more obvious political suspect. Napoleon, like most dictators, placed the political life of the nation on ice: once the thaw came in 1815 one discovers a resurgence of political activity and violence, not, it is true, on the same scale as 1793 or 1795, but which accounted nonetheless in the South of France for the lives of hundreds of people, including a Napoleonic Marshal and a General. This White Terror, which affected in the main the departments of the South-East, reveals once again the continuing pattern of provincial separatism, personal vendettas, political and religious antagonisms which antedated revolutions and empires. As Catholic children in the Gard innocently chanted:

> *Protestant blood to wash our hands*
> *We cheerfully shall take,*
> *And with the blood of Calvin's sons*
> *Black puddings we shall make*

we appear to have been thrown back to the era of the Religious Wars, of the violent Protestant uprising at the beginning of the eighteenth century known as the *Guerre des Camisards* and the brutal repression of Protestant communities during the following decades. Here again, the Revolutionary and Napoleonic period provides us with striking evidence of the persistence of historical antipathies and antagonisms.

7 The Nation-in-Arms

For almost the entire period covered by this book, France was a nation-in-arms. The demands of war exercised a profound influence on practically every aspect of French life—its government, its economy, its society, even its culture. If the Royal Army had reflected the hierarchy of birth and breeding under the *ancien régime*, the armies of the Revolution and Empire reflected the identification of the people with the nation. Like the Roman emperors he loved to imitate, Napoleon realised only too well the need to provide the French with excitement and *la gloire*. The pageantry and pomp of the fêtes of the Revolution and the grand military parades of the Empire brought a little colour into the rather drab world of the poorer sections of the community: 'The army was the symbol of revolutionary solidarity. It assured not only the territorial integrity of the Republic, but also the survival of the Revolution itself. *La Révolution et son armée forment un bloc.*'

Before 1789, the armed forces of the *ancien régime* had also formed *un bloc*: the social composition of both the Army and the Navy reflected the fundamental antagonism in society between a privileged élite and the mass of the nation. It was extremely difficult for a soldier of poor origins—indeed even for the poorer provincial nobility—to effect an entry into the officer caste. In 1789, out of a total of almost 10,000 army officers, over 6,500 were of noble birth. Regiments could be bought and sold, which did not increase the professional expertise of the force, although the pecuniary aspect was offset by the fact that, for the nobility, the army was in their blood. Madame des Echerolles recalled that her father had been taken off to learn the arts of war at the tender age of nine: her grandfather wishing to acquaint the boy 'at an early age with the strains and the rigorous life of an army camp'.

The Royal Army had been a volunteer force, although a reserve of about 75,000 men—the highly unpopular militia—had been chosen by lot, spending, in peace-time, a few weeks a year in training. The really crack regiments had formed part of the King's Household, a force of over 7,000 men, whereas the bulk of the army, numbering over 250,000 and divided into the cavalry, artillery and infantry, had been drawn from the lowest section of the population. The towns had always provided more recruits, proportionally, than the country-side: the recruiting-sergeant could use the lure of 'wine, women and song' and, of course, better wages to more effect in the towns than in the countryside where the peasant's attachment to the soil and his community was proverbial. One of the distinguishing features of the Royal Army had been its cosmopolitan composition, with Italians, Swiss, Germans and Irish providing a high proportion of the total number of troops. It is perhaps fitting that when the Monarchy finally fell on 10 August 1792 it should have been defended in its last hours by a detachment of Swiss Guards.

On the eve of the Revolution, the spirit, if not the composition of the army was changing rapidly. Many of the officer corps had been infected with the ideas of the Enlightenment, ideas derived in some instances—as was the case with the marquis de Lafayette—from America where many troops had fought in the War of Independence. The dissemination of those ideas which helped to precipitate a revolutionary crisis had their impact on the armed forces as on any other section of the community. In June 1789, the Gardes-Françaises regiment in Paris was heard to shout 'Vive le Tiers', whilst in October of the same year the Flanders regiment, stationed at Versailles, refused to fire on the crowd. Slowly the armature of the monarchy was being stripped away.

The early years of the Revolution completed the disintegration of the army, giving birth to a new force based on a cause rather than a class. The National Guard and the Volunteers of 1791–2 transformed the military might of France into a national revolutionary army. During the early years of the Revolution, soldiers and sailors alike began to challenge the old military values and traditions. At naval bases like Toulon and Brest sailors mutinied, causing serious embarrassment in government circles. The Constituent Assembly was obliged to follow a middle course between conceding many of the demands of the increasingly politicised rank-and-file and maintaining an armed force capable of defending France and the Revolution. In August 1790, a law was passed to prevent acts of insubordination and, in the same month, the government sanctioned the severely repressive measures taken by the marquis de Bouillé in crushing the rebellion of the Chateauvieux regiment at Nancy. In September, soldiers were forbidden to join political societies; six months later the law had to be rescinded. Confronted with the impossibility of separating military life from a revolutionary situation, most army and navy officers became increasingly isolated. A few had emigrated at the beginning of the Revolution: over 2,000 (out of a total of 9,500) left in the summer of 1791 after the failure of the King's flight from Varennes. Of 727 naval officers above the rank of lieutenant, in 1791, only 400 were left a year later. At the same time, the Assembly was debating the demand for a levy of 100,000 volunteers. The *armée du métier* was rapidly being superseded by a truly national force.

The National Guard, which was to provide many of the early volunteers, had originally been formed in the critical summer months of 1789. It was destined to play an important role in every Parisian revolution until the Commune of 1871. Conceived as a defensive force against any possible counter-attack by the Court, it was also regarded by many as an insurance policy against an increasingly vocal, if not

58 '*The Nation-in-Arms*'

ARMÉE PARISIENNE.

Grenadier   Fusillier   Chasseur   Sappeur   Canonier   Piqu

altogether articulate, *classe populaire*. A letter from the wife of a deputy to her fourteen-year-old son, dated 6 September 1789, accurately reflects the dual role played by the National Guard, at least during the opening years of the Revolution. Commenting on recent disturbances in the capital, she noted that, 'our brave representatives, having triumphed over the evils of despotism, will never allow themselves to be intimidated by the threats of an unruly mob. If they try to go too far, the hero who is at the head of the National Guard, knows full well how to deal with them'. Her 'hero' was the marquis de Lafayette, a liberal noble, but who, like so many other 'liberal nobles', was to go over to the enemy in 1792. Only *active* citizens (those who paid taxes equivalent to the value of three days work) were to be eligible for service in the National Guard, according to the law of May 1790, and since the recruit had to find his own uniform—royal blue with scarlet and white trimmings—and weapons, the composition of the Guard up to 1792 was almost exclusively bourgeois. Almost exclusively, since it was by no means unknown for members of the aristocracy to be invited to command detachments of the National Guard, a tribute to their military expertise and the fact that they were quite frequently, alongside the curé, the natural leaders of the community.

The summer of 1791, which saw the increasing, if as yet hesitant, interference of other European powers in France's internal affairs, witnessed a more positive effort to provide the government with an army and navy capable of meeting the impending threat of war. An appeal for 100,000 Volunteers was launched and, although not exactly over-subscribed, the response was encouraging. The inducements offered to the Volunteers help to explain why in the towns and cities of France so many artisans and day-labourers responded to the appeal. At a time when work was not easy to find, the prospect of fifteen sous a day pay (far more than the regular soldier received), relaxed discipline and, perhaps most important of all, the knowledge that the term of service was for one year only, did not prove unattractive. A Volunteer army also offered a wonderful opportunity for rapid advancement to the trained soldier who had been denied preferment under the *ancien régime*.

The scarcely-veiled hostility with which the 'whites', or regular soldiers, viewed the 'blues', or Volunteer forces, was often aggravated

59　*An army recruiting-stand at the beginning of the Revolution*

by the behaviour of the latter during the opening campaigns of the war against Austria and Prussia in the spring of 1792. Badly trained and equipped, occasionally very poorly led, the Volunteers, after a few initial successes in Belgium, were soon taking to their heels, hurling accusations of treason against all and sundry and massacring a General in Lille for good measure. By the summer of 1792, the situation had become critical. The fall of the fortress town of Longwy had opened up the road to Paris. It was against this background that the storming of the Tuileries occurred on 10 August and, three weeks later, the September Massacres.

The popular response evoked by the announcement of *la patrie en danger* swept the sans-culottes into the Popular Societies, the National Guard and into the army. Forty thousand Volunteers enlisted in the frontier departments, a further 20,000 marching from Paris in September to halt the Prussian advance. The reason that they did not play a more active role in the famous battle of Valmy, which turned the tide of the war and hence of the Revolution, can be explained less by any lack of enthusiasm on the part of the Volunteers than the hesitancy of Generals who preferred to rely on more seasoned troops buttressed by some battalions of the 1791 Volunteers. The fact that, whether in reserve or in the front line, regular and volunteer troops had fought together in one of the great battles of the Revolution did a great deal to fuse together these two distinct halves of France's military power. In the summer of 1793, Volunteers and Regulars were to be officially amalgamated—forty Volunteers and twenty Regulars being assigned to each company.

Success at Valmy was followed by a series of victories culminating in the conquest of Belgium by Dumouriez in the winter of 1792. For many of the Volunteers, this success made it easier for them, despite patriotic appeals from the Government, to retire from the army, as they were entitled to do, in December. Only a month or so later, the scope of the war widened considerably with the declaration of war on the Republic by Great Britain. The favourable military situation was gradually reversed until, by the early summer of 1793, the situation was almost as critical as it had been a year earlier. The outbreak of the counter-revolution in the Vendée in March 1793, the federalist revolt a few months later, the military reversals in the North-East and the Pyrenees, all forced the Government to take drastic action.

On 21 February 1793, the Government had introduced the first of a series of measures designed to save the Revolution—the levy of 300,000 conscripts. In August of the same year, Barère announced the principle of the *levée en masse*: 'that every Frenchman is requisitioned for the service of the nation'. The harnessing of all human and material resources against the Allied Powers led stage by stage to the rise of the Jacobins, the inauguration of the Terror, the introduction of a controlled economy and the mass participation of the people in the Revolution. Whatever theories, Rousseauist or otherwise, the Jacobins invoked to justify their rule, they were, at least until the spring of 1794, incidental to the one major objective—the struggle for survival. Under the leadership of Lazare Carnot and Jeanbon Saint-André, in charge of the army and navy respectively, the Republic was destined not only to

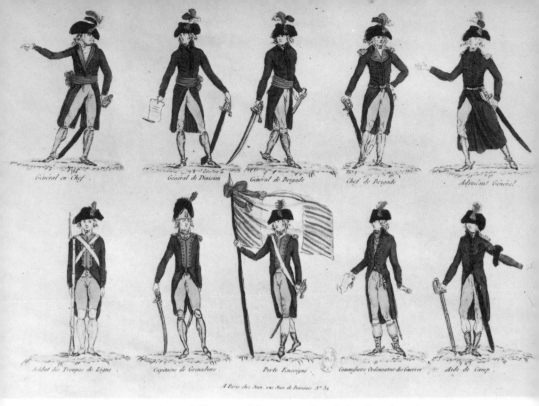

Général en Chef .   Général de Division .   Général de Brigade .   Chef de Brigade .   Adjudant Général .

Soldat des Troupes de Ligne .   Capitaine de Grenadiers .   Porte Enseigne .   Commissaire Ordonnateur des Guerres .   Aide de Camp .

À Paris chez Jean, rue Jean de Beauvais N° 34

60   *Officers and lower ranks of the Regular Army*

survive but to carry the flag of the Revolution to most continental
countries, thus preparing the way for the memorable victories of
Napoleon Bonaparte.

The success of the Republican and Napoleonic armies was due in
no small measure to changes introduced, or at least first discussed,
during the *ancien régime*. In 1772, the comte de Guibert had published,
anonymously in London, his work on tactics which first outlined the
need for a modern national army. Four years later, Gribeauval had
introduced his new cannon which was to remain the basic unit of
fire-power used by the French until 1830. Finally, in 1786, the marquis
de Castries had formulated his plans, as Minister of the Marine, for
a reorganised navy. It should also be remembered that many of the
great military figures of the period had received their early baptism of
fire before the Revolution. What the Revolution itself did was to provide

the manpower, the dynamism and the opportunity for the military potential of France to be realised.

The enthusiasm of the Volunteers forced the strategy of the army into a more offensive mould. The army began to rely more on light infantry and the use of the column as opposed to the time-honoured square of three ranks (only the first two actually being engaged in battle). But perhaps the most important change was the reliance placed upon the artillery, particularly by Napoleon, who used it increasingly to destroy the enemy's confidence before launching a main attack—a principle which was still being followed over a century later. In 1801, the army had only 20,000 *canonniers*; by 1814, this figure had risen to over 80,000. Contrary to popular belief Napoleon did not, before the Russian campaign in 1812, place great reliance on massive armies. What he sought, and what he obtained, was remarkable mobility and flexibility. Napoleon fought each battle according to circumstances, possibly his greatest asset being the selfless devotion of his officers and the quite incredible loyalty, amounting in some cases to veneration, of the soldier in the ranks.

The navy, lacking a military genius like Napoleon, hardly altered its tactics and strategy at all during this period. Consisting of over sixty vessels of the line and as many frigates in 1793, it was qualitatively, particularly from the point of view of fire-power, if not quantitatively better than its main rival, the British fleet. Ideas concerning a possible invasion of Britain, or bringing her to her knees by blockading her exports, continued to exercise a fatal fascination for naval planners from 1793 to the end of the Empire. It is true that, apart from Jeanbon Saint André's work in 1793, the Government never provided the same funds or generated the same enthusiasm for the navy as for the army, whilst, all too often, internal considerations, such as the war in the Vendée, seriously restricted its objectives. The French navy could never quite master the tactics of the British fleet, as the battle in June 1794 illustrated when the *Vengeur*, after a truly heroic encounter with the *Brunswick*, was sunk with the loss of 350 men. After the crushing defeat of Trafalgar in October 1805—as a consequence of which only eleven battered hulks survived out of a combined Spanish and French fleet of thirty-three ships—any ideas about the control of the Channel were dispelled for good and Napoleon became entirely

61 *The brave but unavailing resistance of the* Vengeur *in 1794 was rapidly transformed into legend*

absorbed in a continental strategy which involved closing the ports of Europe to British goods.

The period of the Revolution and Empire produced greater social mobility between the various classes than at any time before, or indeed after. In no sphere of life was this mobility better exemplified than in the army. Few would have believed in 1789 that a lawyer's son named Bernadotte, who had enlisted as a regular soldier would have become King of Sweden; or that a cadet officer from Corsica named Buonaparte would have been elevated to the exalted position of Emperor of the French. Many of Napoleon's Generals and Marshals came from even more obscure origins: Rossignol had been an apprenticed goldsmith, Lefebvre was the son of a joiner (he married a washerwoman), Lannes the son of an ostler.

One of Napoleon's greatest Marshals was Massena who had gone to sea as a cabin-boy at the age of thirteen. His subsequent career was certainly not unique amongst the officer corps. Joining the Royal-

Italian regiment in 1779, he left the army ten years later having been refused a commission. The outbreak of the Revolution found him in charge of a grocer's shop, but then, like so many other experienced soldiers, he was offered the post of Captain of the National Guard. Enlisting in the Volunteer army of 1791, he had reached the rank of Divisional-General by 1794. By the time Napoleon had seized power, Massena was commanding the Army of Italy. Napoleon raised the status of the soldier, not just of the officer, although he was not un-favourable to the claims of aristocratic birth. The great majority of the 48,000 *Légions d'Honneur* went to soldiers.

Having attained their privileged position, the majority of Napoleon's officer corps lived in a style becoming their station in life; indeed Napoleon insisted that they should. Murat, a Marshal at the age of thirty-five, had the dubious good fortune to marry Napoleon's sister Caroline, living in palatial splendour as co-ruler of Southern Italy. Others only slightly less fortunate, were given estates and chateaux together with funds to finance them. Massena bought a chateau ten

62   *One of the heroic episodes in Napoleon's military career which helped bring him to power*

63 *Massena – one of Napoleon's most talented generals*

miles from Paris which had once been the home of Cardinal Richelieu. Berthier loved to surround himself with young nobles—his dandies—which gave a touch of old world charm to his camp. Many of the *aides-de-camps* of the Napoleonic armies were in fact sons of nobles, a few like Marmont reaching the highest positions in the army. Napoleon was not too interested in their pedigree so long as they did their job well, and that usually meant doing what they were told. On the field of battle, many high-ranking officers shared the privations of the ordinary trooper, sleeping in the open, leading their men by examples of personal courage and daring. Undoubtedly, much of this enthusiasm had died by the end of the Empire: having survived twenty years of warfare, amassing, in many cases, huge personal fortunes the former 'hammers of the aristocracy' were in serious danger of becoming aristocrats themselves.

The problem of finding enough recruits to staff the armies became more difficult as the strategy of war changed from the defensive to the offensive. The original volunteer system having proved inadequate, the Government had introduced the principle of conscription. First enunciated on 14 February 1793, it was extended in August by the famous declaration of the *levée en masse*, according to which all citizens, women and children included, were to regard themselves as being in the service of the nation. Never before had the State made such sweeping demands on its subjects, as the rebels in the Vendée were quick to point out. The principle of conscription was confirmed by the law of 5 September 1798 which remained in force throughout the Empire. Conscription produced the massive armies of the period: in 1794, the Republic had over one million men under arms, four times the size of the prerevolutionary army. From 1801 to 1815, no fewer than one-and-a-half million more Frenchmen were called upon to serve the cause of the Revolution.

64   *This trumpeter, like other members of Napoleon's officer corps, lived in a style becoming his noble background*

Needless to say, conscription was not popular in France: it evoked all too painful memories of the militia. In the West, conscription helped to provoke the massive uprising against the Republic. Almost immediately the law of conscription was circulated, placards appeared mysteriously promising 'Woe to those who preach conscription'. Clearly it was bad enough being told by people from the towns that they should live for the Revolution; dying for it was going too far. The fact that only bachelors were expected to serve in the armies meant that many a marriage was contracted in haste, doubtless to be represented at leisure. In 1809, the marriage rate in Paris rose by almost fifty per cent. Resistance was most pronounced in the poorer agricultural areas where farmers could ill afford to lose their sons. To avoid the draft, birth certificates were falsified (often with the connivance of the local curé), sons mysteriously 'died' and men shot off their fingers or knocked out their teeth so that they would be incapable of firing or loading a rifle.

Desertions became one of the principle headaches of the Government. In March 1795, France had more than 1,100,000 men officially enrolled in the army. However, it was estimated that not more than one-half of this number were actually under arms. General Kellerman was moved to comment that, 'if these desertions continue, there will only be the officer corps left to serve'. In 1803, out of a total of 220 conscripts who were required to report for duty at the place des Vosges in Paris, only sixty-three bothered to turn up. The prefect of the Var reported in March 1805 that of the 611 original conscripts in his department, over a hundred had already deserted.

The problem became more acute as Napoleon was obliged to increase his demands for manpower. Under the Consulate, an average of 50,000 men a year were being drafted; in 1808 this figure had risen to 160,000, by 1812 to 280,000. From 1791 to 1813, the total number of men who had served in the French armies was no fewer than 4,500,000. The problem of brigandage, which plagued France under the Directory and again towards the end of the Empire, was related to the high rate of desertion. It also helps to explain the sympathy of local populations for *les brigands*: very often, it was their own sons they were protecting. As is customary, it was the poor who were forced to bear the brunt of the fighting. The rich could, by the provisions of the law of 5 September

65   *Balloons were used to decide the deployment of troops by the French Army at the Battle of Fleurus in 1794*

1798, buy themselves out of the draft, although the cost of finding a replacement rose from 2,000 francs at the beginning of the Empire to 12,000 by 1812.

For those who made the army their life—and many preferred it to civilian life—there was the share of glory which was associated with belonging to the finest armies in Europe. They rarely forgot that they were soldiers of liberty, retaining something of the spontaneity of the early Volunteers. A letter sent in 1793 by Joliclerc, a Volunteer in the 7th battalion of the Var regiment, reflects something of this spirit: 'the principles of love for my country, for freedom and for the Republic are not just written, but indelibly imprinted upon my heart and will remain so long as it pleases that Supreme Being who governs all to leave one breath of life in my body'; or, in more prosaic terms, a comment from Gilbert, a Volunteer in the Allier battalion writing at the time of Valmy: 'The enemy are not invulnerable; they have more experience, but we have more courage'. Although this early enthusiasm was probably felt only by a small minority, much of it having disappeared by 1794, the army always retained a consciousness of its unique role as the repository of revolutionary ardour and enthusiasm. This feeling extended from the lowest ranks to the highest. General Marmont wrote in his memoirs: 'I felt as if I had been transported to another sphere. At 55, I still feel that intensity and enthusiasm as if it were yesterday'. The hardened professional soldier, the *grognard* of the Empire, was easily recognisable—arrogant, noisy, a connoisseur of wine, women and licentious song.

Despite the patriotism and the glory which informed the spirit of the armies, life was extremely hard, dangerous and often boring. Recruits spent but a brief time in the barracks—usually a converted church or monastery—learning the rudiments of warfare before being posted to their regiments. Once on a campaign, most of their life would be spent in the open, but if the regiment were stationed for a long spell in one spot, as at Boulogne preparing for the invasion of England which never materialised, a makeshift but fairly comfortable camp could be constructed. They might be fortunate enough to be lodged in the house of some wealthy bourgeois with their stomachs—not infrequently their beds—filled, but such luxuries tended to be exceptional. Joliclerc, writing to his mother in October 1793, complained, 'I have been here for several months, sleeping on the same patch of ground and wearing the same uniform'.

In 1794, the Seventh battalion marched from Brest to Switzerland, a distance of 1,200 kilometres, in under two months. Nothing could equal the agony of the army during the retreat from Moscow in 1812 when, suffering from the intense cold and the harassment of the Cossacks, they were forced to drink the blood of their own horses. In January of the same year, after three months with little food, a battalion near Talavera in Spain, 'was reduced to such an extremity that our soldiers, receiving only two ounces of rice a day, were forced to live off roots and the huge thistles which are very common in these parts'. As one soldier scratched on a wall in Italy: 'To be a good soldier one has to have the heart of a lion, the feet of a mountain goat and the stomach of an ant.'

Since the French armies, particularly under Napoleon, relied on

66   *The Russian retreat, 3 November 1812*

rapid movement to gain the all-important element of surprise, it was inevitable that the soldiers should have been forced to live off the land. The French were certainly not more undisciplined than their enemies, quite the contrary. In 1793, the Convention passed a law which included the death penalty for indiscriminate pillage and repeated desertion, and officers occasionally invoked it in order to set an example to their men. Marshal Davout was particularly strict on pillagers. Given, however, that regular supplies—like wages—were often lacking, soldiers had little alternative but to pillage in order to live. Parts of Saxony were ravaged after the battle of Jéna and during the terrible retreat from Moscow what alternative was there for the soldier but to seize anything on which he could lay his hands? Rome was sacked by French troops after the declaration of the Republic in February 1798—hardly an auspicious start for the fledgling state! On this occasion, as on many others, Massena turned a blind eye to the proceedings, or rather an eye dazzled by his own loot from the Italian campaign, estimated at well over two million francs. Chevillet, a musician, summed it up: 'When one wages war in enemy country one takes what there is to take . . . the desire for gain forms part of the

67   *(Overleaf) Napoleon's army crossing the St Bernard Pass*

make-up of a soldier. The alternative is to be poor and miserable, with the ever present threat of death hanging over one's head'.

Not that it was always the enemy who suffered from the depredations of the army. Most mayors and prefects were obliged at some time or another to face deputations of angry citizens complaining about the conduct of troops garrisoned in their locality. In December 1794, the mayor of a little commune in Brittany was induced to send off an irate letter to the Government bitterly denouncing the behaviour of a group of soldiers who had attacked a peasant before walking off with some of his produce. Pillage, accompanied at times by drunkenness and rape, was all too readily accepted as the unofficial wages of the soldier. Popular reactions to the invading French in Spain and Germany were not unconnected with the conduct of the troops during their stay in these countries.

Yet no government of the time could have done more to ensure that the army was supplied. From 1793 to 1814, the French people were in a state of almost permanent requisition. On 14 November 1793, Saint Just, disgusted at the terrible conditions which existed in the hospitals of Strasbourg, informed the municipality that, 'it must find in the next twenty-four hours, 2,000 beds to be taken from the wealthy for the use of the Army'. Forced loans were constantly being levied on the rich, particularly during the Terror, plate and bells were taken from churches, horses and carts from the peasantry. The victories of the army in 1794 were only made possible by conscription, requisition and the virtual nationalisation of war matériel.

France had truly become a nation-in-arms. Visitors to the Tuileries or the Luxembourg gardens in Paris would have reacted, not to the refined conversation of the rich or to nannies taking their charges for a morning stroll, but to the hammering of hundreds of improvised forges turning out bullets, rifles and even cannons. Every citizen was asked to search his cellar or his out-houses for saltpetre, essential in the manufacture of gunpowder at this time. At the beginning of 1794, long lines of sans-culottes stood before the bar of the Convention offering up their urns of saltpetre like incense before some new and terrible deity. Under Napoleon, far more reliance was placed on the traditional sources of supplies—the bankers and war-contractors who made vast fortunes out of the Emperor's obsession with war.

68   *The search for saltpetre, indispensable in the production of gunpowder,
became one of the most patriotic duties of a citizen*

The ever-mounting casualty lists remind us of the cost, in human
terms, of France's great military success. Of 30,000 men who set out
on the ill-fated Egyptian campaign, over 10,000 died as a result of
their wounds or from the diseases which ravaged the French camps.
Over 600,000 men set out on the road to Moscow in 1812; of this total,
only one-sixth were to return to their families. These are just two of
the more dramatic instances of high casualty figures in this period.
Georges Lefebvre has estimated that not far short of a million men
died in battle from 1800 to 1815. The outriders of war, disease and
cruelty, were always present. In Egypt, typhus, yellow fever, dysentry,
even the plague, decimated French battalions. Over a thousand
soldiers were burned alive when the Russians set fire to a small village
after the battle of Eylau; in Spain, if soldiers were unfortunate enough
to get separated from their detachment, they were sometimes crucified
by being nailed to a wall or door; thousands more died in the terrible
pontons used by the British to imprison captured soldiers. The French
were not loath to retaliate in kind, as the harrowing prints of Goya
bear witness.

69   *Napoleon views the battlefield at Eylau*

Soldiers could expect nothing but the most rudimentary medical
care if they were wounded on the field of battle. There was no infirmary
system until after the battle of Wagram, and then more in theory
than in practice. Each regiment had its surgeon and his assistants,
but with no antiseptics and with alcohol as the only anaesthetic the
death-rate was fearfully high. Surgeons like Percy, Taillefer and Larrey
were undoubtedly highly skilled, but, in the heat of battle, the usual
recourse was amputation of limbs before gangrene killed off the
patient. Larrey once performed 200 amputations in less than twenty-
four hours. Hospitals, when they were available, were overcrowded,
understaffed and usually riddled with vermin and disease.

One can only admire the fortitude and humour with which the seasoned soldier bore these inevitable accompaniments of war. The euphemistic
jargon adopted was a very human response to the harrowing reality
of their daily life: fleas and lice were inevitably referred to as 'grass-
hoppers'; going into battle was 'setting-off for the marriage-feast';
the Scots, with their kilts were known as 'les vrais sans-culottes'. The

soldier also had more physical and humane consolations. Alongside or behind every army straggled a long line of females, some of them prostitutes, others washerwomen and provisioners of food and drink for soldiers with enough ready cash to pay for such luxuries. These women, often extremely courageous, could be found in the heat of the battle with their little barrels of brandy giving aid and encouragement to the troops. Many were married and it was not unusual for babies to be born as their fathers fought for their own lives in the front ranks. Napoleon realised the value of these *vivandières*, but, as always, sought to bureaucratise them. Each was made to wear a little plaque with her profession and registered number inscribed. Prostitutes—an unofficial profession with the armies—were exempt. Women, of high and low birth, from Massena's mistress who accompanied him to Portugal, to 'Marie tête de bois', killed towards the end of the Empire after surviving seventeen campaigns, fulfilled an indispensable role in the life of the soldier.

It was during the Revolution and Empire that the French reached the peak of their military greatness. Never again would the French armies be in a position to make and unmake states as they had done in this period. The prerequisites of greatness were changing. Nevertheless, the victories of Valmy, Marengo, Jéna and Austerlitz, purged by time and legend of a million dead, of the misery and privation which so often characterised the ordinary soldier's life, form an integral part of the evolution of modern French history.

8　The Artist in an Age of Revolution

Revolutions present problems to the artist in any age. Reflecting in his work something of the morals and values of the society in which he lives, it is inevitable that he should be regarded with suspicion by political leaders and factions. The Jacobins were particularly concerned about the projection of their image: 'la vertu' was in vogue; vice (*les moeurs aristocratiques*) was denounced by politicians and artists alike. The great actor, Larive, found himself reduced to walk-on parts in the prison of the Port-Libre; one of the finer poets of the period, André Chénier, was executed under the Terror. Napoleon Bonaparte was equally concerned that the journalist, the actor and the painter should produce images in his own likeness. The debate, first launched by the Encyclopedia and in particular by Diderot, as to the social— and therefore in a revolutionary context, the political function of art— assumed far greater meaning as successive revolutionary governments began to appreciate the significance of art as propaganda.

70　*The Emperor pays homage to the great painter David*

71 *A newspaper stand during the Revolution*

It is also true that most societies produce two separate cultures—one for the élite, another for the masses. This was peculiarly evident during the Revolution and Empire. While most artists and governments favoured neo-classical themes, the mass of the people sought after more frivolous, more exciting and more colourful entertainment. Napoleon might laud the neo-classical paintings of David, or affect a profound interest in the plays of Racine or Corneille, but the majority of his subjects preferred to patronise the pantomimes, the burlesque comedies of the boulevard theatres and the fairs, or book a seat to see one of Pixérécourt's new *melodrames*, or (if they could read) buy one of the many romantic novels which were so popular under the Empire. As the ruling élite clung to the dying forms of the classical revival, the people began to turn increasingly to Romanticism. It is significant that two of the great romantic writers of the period—Chateaubriand and Madame de Stael—both fell into disfavour under the Empire.

Lacking the modern means of communication—radio, television and the cinema—it was through the pulpit, the public orator and the printed word that the Revolution conveyed its message. The pulpit, was virtually closed down by 1794, while the Press was given hitherto undreamed-of freedom. Napoleon reversed the process, requiring the clergy to disseminate carefully-chosen information among the mass of the people, but drastically curtailing the freedom of the Press. Although the Press was still in its infancy—the *Journal de Paris*, the most influential pre-revolutionary paper, had fewer than 10,000 subscribers—the Revolution was to play an important part in its subsequent rapid growth.

Literally hundreds of newspapers and broad-sheets, reflecting the entire political spectrum from the scabrous pages of Hébert's popular and crude *Père Duchesne* to the occasionally pornographic and always counter-revolutionary *Ami des Apôtres*, were rushed onto the street-stalls of the *marchands des journaux*. Hébert's flair for the theatre assisted him in his journalistic mimicry of the popular idiom; his paper also played a significant role in articulating the growing political awareness of the sans-culotterie. Since less than half the populace was literate, such newspapers, supplemented by the most effective of all revolutionary media, the placard, were frequently read out to the illiterate on building sites or in markets by persons specifically chosen and paid for the task.

Papers like the *Père Duchesne*, and particularly in the countryside, the *Feuille Villageoise*, contributed to the dissemination of anti-clerical

72 *Hébert adopted a folk-hero—the Père Duchesne – as the image for his popular newspaper*

73 *The Père Duchesne angrily uncovers yet another plot against the people!*

MEMENTO MORI

Je suis le véritable pere Duchesne, foutre!

La Grande Colere

DU

PERE DUCHESNE,

De voir l'Assemblée Nationale s'amuser à la moutarde, tandis que les Brigands couronnés nous préparent un coup de chien abominable. Découverte d'une grande conspiration de ces mangeurs d'hommes, pour renverser notre Constitution & faire égorger tous les Patriotes.

DÉFIONS-nous de l'eau qui dort, foutre. Plus nos ennemis font les chiens couchans, plus nous devons les redouter. Ils ne nous donneront

74 *Diogenes and Marat, both sans-culottes, both persecuted for speaking the truth! The revival in classical studies exerted a powerful influence on the art and rhetoric of the Revolution*

doctrines. Others, like the widely-read *Ami du Peuple* of Jean-Paul Marat, encouraged popular demands for violence and justice. For some weeks before the September Massacres, Marat had been advocating in the *Ami du Peuple* the execution of a few hundred 'aristocrates' in order to rid France of traitors. Like Marat, Prudhomme, the editor of the *Revolutions de Paris*, frequently invoked classical references to sanction his political arguments. Such a device might be adopted to make violence respectable, as in no. 214 of the *Révolutions* which noted that, 'The two Brutus's were truly sans-culottes: the elder embraced his son as he condemned him to death; the younger wept on the breast of his father as he plunged in his dagger'. No doubt Robespierre, with tears in his eyes but recognising *vertu* when he saw it, would have applauded such sentiments.

There had been some censorship by the Jacobins, even more under the Directory, but it was only during the Empire that the Press was really brought under control. When Napoleon came to power, Paris could boast of over seventy papers; in less than a year this figure had been reduced to thirteen and by the end of the Empire, effectively to four. At the same time, the number of newspapers in the departments was reduced to one, and even this had to reproduce the government line as laid down in the official Moniteur. A government department was created to deal with the censorship of letters, books and newspapers which proved far more efficient than the corresponding institution had been under the *ancien régime*. If the average Frenchman became bored—as the majority must have done—with the predictability of his daily newspaper, he could supplement his reading matter with a glance through Napoleon's Bulletins which recorded the exploits of France's military machine. First appearing in 1805, the Bulletins, which, alongside the Bible, were to be found on most church lecterns, continued to be published until 1812 when, for obvious reasons, it was thought wiser to discontinue them.

Napoleon, who was not opposed to people thinking so long as their political thought ran along Imperial lines, did not interfere with the re-emergence of literary societies and journals after 1800. The most influential publication dealing with the arts and the sciences was *La Décade*, the journal of the *Idéoloques* edited by Pierre-Louis Guinquené. *La Décade* was Voltairian in inspiration, strongly anti-clerical, but its political manifesto was confined to a few soothing comments on the desirability of spreading 'patriotic, civic and fraternal sentiments'. Had it been more precise it would undoubtedly have been

banned. Articles, some contributed by the leading literary critic Geoffroy, others by Jean-Baptiste Say, the influential economist, preached
the manifold virtues of the nascent industrial age, extolling the marvels
of science, machines and the benefits to be derived from a laissez-faire
system. One's moral and ethical behaviour—according to Guinquené
—should be dictated by motives of enlightened egoism. All the classical
tenets of nineteenth-century Liberalism, its vices and its virtues, were
readily accessible to any reader of *La Décade*. The journal was truly
representative of its period, reflecting the opinions of the enlightened
bourgeois standing on the threshold of a new era, marvelling, like a
child, at its obvious attractions, but ignorant of, or blind to its equally
apparent dangers.

Almost as important as the Press in propagandising the virtues of
the Revolution were the scores of theatres which flourished during the
Revolution, again to be drastically curtailed by Napoleon. The French
theatre had won a deservedly famous reputation long before the
Revolution. The English traveller, Arthur Young, was extremely
impressed by its quality and style, both in Paris and the provinces. The
Comédie-Française and the *Théâtre des Italiens*, both benefiting from a
monopoly of certain types of plays and operas, attracted the best
playwrights and artists in Western Europe. Beaumarchais' *Mariage de
Figaro* proved to be one of the most resounding successes in the immediate prerevolutionary decade. The boulevard theatre was also
becoming increasingly popular in France with many theatres opening—
against stiff opposition from the established institutions—in Paris
and the largest of the provincial towns. In order to circumvent the law
on staging plays which the Comédie considered to be within its private
domain, some managers went as far as placing a transparent gauze
curtain between the actors and the audience.

The Revolution, however, hostile to closed corporations and privileged societies, quickly swept away the monopoly enjoyed hitherto by
the traditional theatres, undoubtedly lowering the quality, but vastly
increasing the quantity and variety of plays, operas and farces available
to the general public. The prestigious cast of the Comédie was soon
divided over their personal political allegiances, some spending a short
spell in prison, others, like the great new actor Talma, supporting the
Jacobins and leading a new group of actors. In 1793, no fewer than 250

75 *Talma – the most famous actor of the Revolutionary and Napoleonic period*

new plays were produced in Paris alone, most of them of very inferior quality. Many of the leading figures in the Popular Movement had been associated with the theatre in one form or another: Hébert had been employed in one, Ronsin, Commander-in-Chief of the Parisian Revolutionary Army, had written some bad plays as had many other figures in and around the Revolutionary Government of the Year II.

Most of the new productions during the early years of the Revolution carried an overt political message. There were plays about honourable collectors of saltpetre, the virtues of a Republican wife, the treachery of Vendean priests and aristocrats, the noble, civic qualities of the son who preferred to see his parents—unrepentant monarchists—imprisoned rather than the Republic endangered. Just as painters regarded the art of the eighteenth century as immoral and decadent so the new generation of revolutionary playwrights saw the theatre as being in need of moral regeneration. Every play should tell a story:

Nos théâtres jadis frivoles,
Desormais seront des écoles
De moeurs et de purs sentiments.

One of the most dramatic and successful Jacobin plays was *Le dernier jugement des rois* in which the King of England, the King of Prussia, the Pope and Catherine the Great were imprisoned on a volcanic desert island. After a few scenes depicting the wickedness of rulers in general, the madness of George III and the nymphomanic character of Catherine the Great (who attempts to seduce the Pope) in particular, this varied collection of temporal and spiritual rulers are finally engulfed by a volcanic eruption. It had the sans-culottes cheering in the aisles.

Typical of the new breed of theatrical managers who, before the Revolution, had tried unsuccessfully to break the monopoly of the older theatres, was Toussaint Mareux, a former manufacturer of mirrors from the Marais quarter of Paris. Mareux had presented his very first *spectacle* on 14 January 1786, but was forced to close down a short time later owing to the opposition of the Comédie-Française. The Revolution brought him a new lease of life, and on 1 October 1789 Mareux was back in business. His théâtre Saint-Antoine had 390 seats, three tiers of *loges* and an orchestra of twenty-two players. A seat on the ground floor cost twenty-four sous; seven francs was the customary charge for a box in the Dress Circle (although subscribers usually bought seats in blocks of five). Early productions included *Le Cid* and the *Barber of Seville*. Increasingly, however, as the Revolution gained momentum, both the course of Mareux's life and the content of his plays altered. In 1792, Mareux was a member of the Insurrectionary Commune of Paris, an onerous responsibility which led to a slump in the fortunes of his theatre. Mareux soon returned to his theatre and for some years, particularly under the Directory, made a relative success of his productions, although competition was always fierce. Increasingly under the Empire, however, the théâtre Saint Antoine was forced to close for longer and longer periods due to successive financial crises. Like many parvenu theatre managers, Mareux's best days had disappeared with the advent of Napoleon.

The theatres of the Revolution catered for all classes and indeed all tastes. Madame Montansier's establishment in the Palais Royal

76   *A circus at the end of the eighteenth century*

provided young gentlemen, not only with the latest chef d'oeuvre of the theatre, but an attractive choice of young ladies to take home after the final curtain. Elsewhere the popular passion for farces, pantomimes and comic opera was adequately catered for. For the first time in French history the theatre was becoming a way of life for a fairly wide section of urban society. It was a difficult time for actors and managers given the acute political tensions of the period and the attitude of the theatre-goers who tended to identify with every character and word the actor delivered. It was not unusual for actors to be asked to repeat popular passages or to omit unfavourable references to *le peuple* or *la vertu*. Reputations could be destroyed within an hour of the opening curtain with angry audiences invading the stage, a tradition maintained even in the more decorous times of the Empire. In 1812, two out of six new plays produced at the théâtre de la rue de la loi failed to reach the final act.

Napoleon's attitude to the theatre was not dissimilar to that which he revealed towards the Press: it was a useful medium to enhance his personal reputation as well as that of the régime in general. It was certainly not something which should be allowed to pander to the tastes of the vile multitude. Theatres began to disappear like newspapers, the most important factor in their disappearance being the favour shown towards such established and expensive institutions like the Opéra and the Théâtre-Français (the former Comédie-Française). Their monopoly over certain plays was restored and by the law of 1806 the Ministry of Police was given the right to censor all plays and productions intended for the Parisian or provincial theatres. In 1807, the list of theatres officially supported by the Government was reduced to eight.

While Napoleon basked in the reflected glory of Racine or Corneille's classical heroes, the average Frenchman, whose appetite for the theatre had been whetted by the events of the Revolution, refused to allow the more popular theatre to die. In Paris one could still attend the Gaiété or L'Ambigu or even the dozens of private productions which took place in private homes, warehouses or even cellars. In 1810, no fewer than 128 plays were produced in the provinces, apart, that is, from the strolling players who continued to perform in market-places and fairs. Marseilles had three theatres by the end of the Empire, Lyons two, whilst outside the most fashionable of Bordeaux's four theatres queues waited for over four hours to see and hear the now famous Talma in one of his great tragic roles.

Just as the Revolution destroyed the pattern of aristocratic society, so it broke up the forms of the classical theatre. Louis-Sébastien Mercier's plays were written for and attracted a much wider bourgeois audience, just as Kotzebue's productions were doing in Germany: the age of the 'drawing-room comedy' was beginning to replace that of the boudoir. But it was the actor rather than the playwright who dominated the theatre in this period. Talma's insistence on realistic costumes and a much freer delivery of his lines was greeted with derision in his early career; by the end of the Empire this theatrical revolution in dress and expression had largely been accepted. Mlle. Mars, whose portrayals of the *ingenue* evoked lavish praise from the critics, was able to command quite remarkable salaries and an even more remarkable male following; Mlle. Georges, possibly the most famous actress of her day, attracted the attentions of no less a person than the Emperor himself.

Although the great majority of plays written during the Revolution and Empire can be dismissed as 'tracts for the times', there are at least two playwrights who deserve mention—Colin d'Harleville and Guibert de Pixérécourt. The former was probably the most respected playwright of his day. He had made his reputation in the 1780s with such successes as *L'Inconstant* (which was produced for the Court), *L'Optimiste* and *Le Château en Espagne*. D'Harleville was thirty-four when the Revolution broke out and, despite many new plays, he was never again to achieve the level of excellence which he had reached with his pre-revolutionary works. For d'Harleville, as for many other artists, the times were out of joint. He did attempt to 'politicise' his work as with that hymn of praise to the Jacobin Republic, *Rose et Picard*, which was first produced in June 1794; but although it won him his *certificat de civisme* so far as the sans-culottes were concerned, it was hardly great art. A few weeks later, d'Harleville was busily rewriting some of the verses to suit the new political climate—the Robespierreists had been executed in July! D'Harleville's predicament was that of most writers and artists: it was difficult to keep one verse or one brush-stroke ahead of the guillotine. D'Harleville died in 1806, never having recaptured his early popularity.

Guibert de Pixérécourt provides a very different example of the artist in this age. His work (both for the social historian and the student of the theatre) is particularly exciting, as it represents a truly transitional stage between the classical and the romantic. Much of his style, particularly the declamatory passages, remains classical, but his real appeal was to popular heroes and popular emotions—Pixérécourt, 'le Corneille des boulevards'. His personal life, like most of his theatrical work, was melodramatic. Born of an aristocratic family in 1773, he was, at times, forced to hide in ditches during the Terror to avoid the attentions of the *comité de surveillance*. His first real success as a playwright came in 1797 with *Les Petits Auvergnats*, exploiting one of the stock comic characters of eighteenth-century literature, the country bumpkin in the big city. But it was to be his melodramas (fifty-nine of his 120 plays were of this genre) which brought the crowds into the boulevard and provincial theatres: *Rosa, ou l'Hermitage du Torrent*, *Victor, ou l'Enfant de la Forêt*, *Pizzaro et les Conquérants du Pérou* or *Les Mines de Pologne* for which Cherubini provided the music. It was these plays which brought movement, colour and excitement to the *petit peuple* as well as a particular challenge to stage-managers who were obliged to find sound and visual effects to simulate waterfalls, rivers, thunder, volcanic lava and many more natural phenomena.

The *melodrame* had been popular in the eighteenth century but it was Pixérécourt who gave it its modern form, inserting prose and dialect for verse forms and reducing the musical element to a subsidiary role. His plays were disliked by the traditionalists—'this bizarre mixture of heroism and triviality; this contrast between common prose and declamation'—but for the ordinary people it offered not only excitement, the romanticism of far-away places, but also an element of reassurance in a very uncertain age. Pixérécourt's message was fairly simple: that vice should be punished and virtues rewarded. His basic characters were also familiar: the villain soiled by vice, the virtuous damsel— usually in distress—the comic relief and the handsome, brave deliverer.

In *Victor, ou l'Enfant de la Forêt*, Robert, the leader of a brigand gang, meets, from the point of view of the plot, a timely death in the last scene, but dies in a noble manner. The message is spelled out: 'There is a final reckoning when the criminal can no longer draw a veil over his crimes; in his dying moments, only he who has never really separated himself from the paths of honour and virtue finds peace'. Most of the brigands in Pixérécourt's plays were basically good souls led astray by temptation or chance. His audiences were often grateful for this: Pixérécourt knew the popular mind well. By the Bourbon Restoration, his reputation was assured as the 'father of melodrama', although he continued writing until the July Monarchy, the reign of Louis Phillipe between 1830 and 1848.

The theme of escapism is best exemplified in the novels of the period, the best of which—and they were very few—lack any overt political message. Nothing appeared to equal, or even to approach, the mastery of Laclos' *Les Liaisons Dangereuses*. The number of works translated from the German and English authors illustrate the importance of foreign influences on French Romanticism as well as the poor quality of the novel in this period. The two literary exceptions to the reign of mediocrity were of course Madame de Stael and Chateaubriand. The appearance of de Stael's *Delphine* in 1802 was noted by the critics as a landmark in the history of the novel. The *Journal de Paris* stated that

77 *Madame de Stael holds court*

the streets of the capital were empty a day after its publication: everyone was indoors reading *Delphine*. Chateaubriand, who worked as a First Secretary in the French Embassy in Rome until his resignation in protest against the execution of the duc d'Enghien, achieved an even greater success with his *Génie du Christianisme*, a lyrical poem in praise of Catholicism, and *Réné*, both works exerting a strong influence on the development of French Romanticism.

Apart from these honourable exceptions, the field was left to a number of female novelists whose insipid romances reward examination rather as period pieces than great works of art. Madame de Krudener's *Valérie*, Madame Collin's *Claire d'Albe* and (most revealing of all) Madame Guichard's *Eleanora, or the Beautiful Washerwoman* are not likely to be revived in the immediate future. Most of these novels were exaggerated in style, full of lachrymose sentiments, occasionally interspersed with tales of horror, death or the bizarre. Historical novels were also very much in vogue. In 1795, Madame de Genlis, one of the more gifted of these *romancières*, had published a story, *Les Chevaliers du Cygne*, based on the court of Charlemagne; in 1806, she published a more widely read historical novel based on the life of Louis XIV's mistress, Madame de Maintenon. Although allegedly based on fact, the work contained some strange accounts of Madame de Maintenon's voyage as a child to Martinique during which, having apparently died of some obscure disease and about to be consigned to the deep, she was saved for Louis XIV by a farewell embrace from her mother which miraculously brought her to life. On another occasion, the good lady had to be saved from the attentions of a monstrous serpent. It is interesting, however, that this novel, which rehabilitated an historical figure associated with the Monarchy and extreme Catholicism, should have had such relative success under Napoleon. Clearly the times had changed since the days of Hébert and the 'grande colère' of his *Père Duchesne!*

Apart from one or two German novels and plays, those of Kotzebue and in particular Goethe's *Werther* translated in 1804, English authors had the greatest influence on the French literary scene. Throughout our period, Shakespeare continued to be translated and produced on the stage, while the English novelists of the eighteenth century were regarded by critics as worthy of imitation. The critic of the *Décade*,

78 *Rouget de Lisle's* Marseillaise *epitomised the revolutionary and military flavour of the period*

commenting on the excellent dialogue and characterisation of de Stael's *Delphine*, could not help noting his own preference for Fielding's *Tom Jones*, 'a masterpiece of realism, of human understanding, of high spirits and of philosophy'. Fielding was described as 'inimitable'; Richardson as 'immortal'. Even the novels of William Godwin, *Caleb Williams* and *Fleetwood* in particular, were praised for their 'social realism'.

Much the same criticism can be made of the poetry of the period which was all too often imitative and uninspired. There were, of course, the famous revolutionary songs, the *Marseillaise* of Rouget de Lisle, the *Carmagnole* and the *Ça ira,* all peculiarly evocative of a nation-in-arms

79 *Contemporary text and music of la Marseillaise*

and in revolution. Towards the end of the Empire, Béranger was adding a new chapter to the romantic tradition of the *chansonnier*. However, with these exceptions, the poetry of the period continued to be dominated by classical tradition. Most poets found themselves alienated from everything that the Revolution stood for: Chénier ends up on the guillotine; the abbé Delille emigrates soon after the outbreak of the Revolution to return under Napoleon with a poetic apologia of his exile entitled, *La Pitié*. Lacking inspiration in their society, many poets, even the most respected, felt obliged to spend far too much of their time translating the classics of Greek, Roman and English poetry than in producing original work.

It was Virgil who exercised the greatest influence on the most popular poet of the period, popular, that is, in helping to create the classical cultural atmosphere that Napoleon sought to create. The poetry of the abbé Delille reflects his knowledge and love of nature, although it is nature stripped of romance: style takes precedence over inspiration. Delille belongs more to the Age of Pope than that of Wordsworth. In 1800, *Les Hommes des Champs* appeared, a work which did not attract great praise, to be followed three years later by *La Pitié*. Apart from his translation of Virgil and Milton, Delille is best remembered—if at all—for his *Chants* and *Odes*. The *Chants* reveal him as a pleasing and technically competent poet, but, at times, banal beyond belief, as with his lines in praise of coffee:

> *Que j'aime a prépare*
> *Ton nectar précieux.*
> *Nul n'usurpe chez moi,*
> *Ce soin délicieux.*

which belongs more to the world of the modern advertising jingle than to that of great art.

Poetry does not reflect the clash between the Romantic and the Classical so clearly as the prose and drama of the period: the influence of poets like Lebrun—the Pindar of the Empire—and Delille was too great to be successfully challenged. What such poetry does illustrate is the wide gap between the 'official' and the 'popular' cultures of the period. Much the same was true of music. It was the traditional and regional folk-song and ballad which characterised popular culture, along with the revolutionary *chants* and such lasting favourites as

Il pleut petite bergère. The Revolution and Empire produced no great music: it is perhaps significant that it took a German, Beethoven, to extol in suitably symphonic form the heroic exploits of Napoleon. Grétry, although the most admired composer of his times, never produced anything to match his *Richard, Coeur de lion* which was first played in Paris in 1784. Méhul was much admired for his religious works, but again it was not a Frenchman who composed the music for Napoleon's coronation, it was Cherubini, an Italian by birth and training. As with the theatre, it was the 'singer not the song' which appeared to attract audiences. Singers like the prima donna Dugazon or the famous tenor, Garat, as well as dancers like Vestris were idolised by Parisians.

It is also true, although less obviously so, that painting is dominated from 1789 to 1815 by classical forms and traditions. Just as Delille influenced poetry, so one man, Jacques-Louis David, presided over the world of the painter. David, nephew of the famous eighteenth-century artist, Boucher, had been sent to study in Rome in 1775. It was there, like so many other late eighteenth-century artists, that he rediscovered the art of the Renaissance. The experience was to exert a profound effect on the remainder of his artistic life. The work of David reminds us once again that revolutions are serious affairs. The concern of the Jacobin for *la vertu* can more readily be understood if we place him in his cultural environment, for the Jacobin only reflected, or perhaps refracted, in political terms what was becoming increasingly a matter of great concern to the artist. If the plays and novels of the second half of the eighteenth century were being criticised for their frivolity and vice, the paintings of Watteau, Boucher and Fragonard were, to David and his school, nothing short of criminal. Art should not be prostituted in order to produce pretty landscapes, royal mistresses in the nude, or even charming young ladies on garden swings. The colour, the charm, the avowed sensuality of eighteenth-century painting was transformed by David into a more sombre, far more moralistic exercise as illustrated by *Le Serment des Horaces* or *Brutus,* both of which appeared in the 1780s. David's art was deceptively simple, austere and neo-classical, concentrating more on the individual than on his environment. Fragonard lived for seventeen years after the outbreak of the Revolution, virtually a forgotten man.

If David did not prostitute his art, he was certainly prepared to politicise it. As 'Pageant-master of the Republic', David was responsible for all the great fêtes and celebrations which characterised the early years of the Revolution. His presentation of these great events provides us with that perfect symbiosis of art, republican *vertu* and neo-classicism which had so concerned Diderot and which much of David's work had already proclaimed. It was rather fortunate that, given his intimate relationship with the Revolutionary Government of the Year II, David survived the reaction which followed the downfall of the Robespierreists. From 1795 on, he dedicated himself to painting, inspiring from his workshop in the *église de Cluny* near the Sorbonne a new generation of painters. The *Death of Marat*, perhaps his most famous painting, reveals quite clearly his debt to the Renaissance, and to Michaelangelo in particular; his huge canvas of Napoleon's coronation reveals a surprising facility for accommodating himself to any régime. The title 'premier peintre de l'Empire', however, was well-merited, both on the grounds of his artistic genius and his willingness

80 *David's portrait of the young Napoleon*

to turn out an entire army of Greeks and Romans on canvas, thus providing yet another cultural buttress for the Imperial façade of Napoleon.

Although some of David's work prefigures the new school of Romanticism, it was left in the main to his disciples to construct, as Pixérécourt had done for the theatre, an effective bridge between the art of the eighteenth and that of the nineteenth century. Gros, the most gifted of David's pupils, produced works less sombre in mood and colour than that of David, as the sensitive portrayal of the young Napoleon illustrates. The paintings of Gérard, Prud'hon and Géricault, although stamped with the neo-classical style of their master, foreshadow the work of a man who was just beginning to make his genius felt at the end of the Empire, a leading exponent of the new Romantic style, Eugène Delacroix.

In the realm of sculpture and architecture it was again classicism which dominated. Most works of art tended to be on the grand scale: 'le gigantesque entrait dans les habitudes'. Canova's sculpture of Napoleon, which, for a variety of reasons, took nearly seven years to complete, was certainly on the grand scale, but a little too classical for the Emperor. A nude Bonaparte was more than Napoleon's rather bourgeois attitudes could accept: his sister Pauline was far more accommodating to the artist in this respect. Canova, really an Italian artist, was given a seat in the French Senate, an example of the 'Europeanisation', or rather the 'Imperialisation' which Napoleon loved to foster. The idea was a spurious one: the satellite countries like Holland, Italy and Western Germany found that for their works of art, as for their goods, all roads led to Paris. The works of indigenous sculptors like Houdon, Chaudet or Despatys were certainly not without merit, but they tended to be overshadowed by the fame of Canova. In architecture, the Paris Bourse designed by Brongniart as well as the elegant hôtels of Percier all emphasise prevailing classical tastes. Doric columns, heavy gilded furniture, lyres, olive-leaves, muses and nymphs were compulsory ornamentation in the homes of the really wealthy.

The artist had undoubtedly suffered during the Revolution and Empire, not so much from political persecution, although this was rarely absent, as from the restrictive, stifling atmosphere produced by fear, flattery and censorship. There was something distinctly 'secondhand' about much of the art of the period; often what was new, original and stimulating was frowned upon by traditionalists and the ruling élite. In Britain popular culture was being seriously threatened, but the mass of the French people, still rural, for whom Classicism or Romanticism were about as remote as the surface of the moon, continued to revel in their traditional pastimes—the *bals populaires*, the village fairs, fêtes and *farandoles*, the *boules* and the bull-fighting in the South, the age-old games described by Rétif de la Bretonne in his autobiographical *Monsieur Nicolas*. The Revolution had provided a stimulating but extremely insecure environment for the artist attempting to satisfy an urban and literate clientele. Napoleon, in his conscious appeal to the past, revealed his limitations as a creative genius, a limitation which he imposed on most artists during the Empire.

Short Glossary

armée révolutionnaire (not to be confused with the Regular Army) volunteers recruited from the ranks of the sans-culottes to propagate the gospel of the Revolution in the countryside—and to ensure grain-supplies to the cities.

assignats paper currency, originally backed by the value of Church Lands placed on the market after 1789.

bonnet rouge the red cap worn by militants, symbolising freedom from slavery.

certificat de civisme documentary proof of revolutionary purity; usually demanded before obtaining employment in the Sections of Paris during the Terror.

comité civil and *comité révolutionnaire* two of the most important committees attached to the Sections of Paris, particularly during the Terror. The former dealt mainly with administrative affairs, the latter, a more important body, had widespread powers of surveillance and arrest.

curé a parish priest, approximating more closely, in clerical rank, to a vicar rather than a curate.

décadi one of the ten days of the week created by the new Revolutionary Calendar introduced in October 1793.

dîme tithe levied by the Catholic Church under the *ancien régime* falling chiefly on crops and varying in incidence from region to region.

émigré a person, not necessarily a noble, who went into exile as a result of his opposition to the Revolution.

incroyables a term used under the Directory to describe people with exaggerated and affected styles of speech and dress.

indigents those whose income, or lack of one, qualified them for assistance from the authorities.

jeunesse dorée pro-royalist youths, identifiable by their garish dress, who delighted in revenging themselves upon the sans-culottes after the collapse of the Terror.

journée a day marking a significant revolutionary insurrection such as the storming of the Bastille on 14 July 1789.

laboureur a wealthy farmer, frequently the leading figure in the village community.

maximum usually referring to the Law of September 1793 which fixed the price of basic food-supplies, particularly bread. The provisions of the Law relating to wages were never imposed with the same rigour.

métayeux a share-cropper, one of the most numerous and the most deprived sections of the French peasantry.

parlements powerful *ancien régime* judicial and administrative institutions—the *parlement* of Paris being by far the most important—which were abolished by the Revolution.

représentants-en-mission agents of the Convention entrusted with considerable powers of repression in the provinces, particularly during the winter of 1793–4.

Revolutionary Government referring to the Jacobin administration of 1793–4 dominated by the Committee of Public Safety and the Committee of General Security.

section originally an administrative and electoral unit—Paris had forty-eight— which was transformed by the sans-culottes after 1792 into an important political organisation.

taille government tax, abolished by the Revolution, which fell most heavily on the peasantry.

Chronological Guide

1787
Feb.   Meeting of Assembly of Notables

1789
April   Réveillon riots in Paris
May   Meeting of the States-General
July   Fall of the Bastille
July–Aug. Widespread peasant insurrections known collectively as the Great Fear
Aug.   National Assembly decrees 'the abolition of feudalism'
Oct.   March to Versailles
Nov.   Nationalisation of Church Lands

1790
July   Civil Constitution of the Clergy

1791
April   Papacy condemns the Civil Constitution of the Clergy
June   Abortive flight of the Royal Family
July   Massacre of the Champs de Mars
Sept.   Dissolution of the National Assembly
Oct.   First Meeting of the Legislative Assembly

1792
April   France declares war on Austria
Aug.   Invasion of the Tuileries leading to the downfall of the Monarchy
Sept.   Prison massacres in Paris
             Battle of Valmy
             First Meeting of the National Convention—Year I of the First French Republic

1793
Jan.   Execution of Louis XVI
Feb.   War declared on Great Britain
March   Creation of the Revolutionary Tribunal
April   Creation of the Committee of Public Safety
June   Invasion of the Convention leading to the rise to power of the Jacobins
Sept.   General Maximum fixing the price of basic food-supplies
Oct.   Introduction of the new Revolutionary Calendar
Dec.   Law of Frimaire institutionalising and centralising the work of the Revolutionary Government

1794
March   Execution of the Hébertists
April   Execution of the Dantonists
June   Fête of the Supreme Being in Paris
             Law of Prairial expediting the work of the Revolutionary Tribunal
             Battle of Fleurus—French armies cross into Belgium
July   Execution of the Robespierrists
Dec.   General Maximum abolished

1795
April–May   Insurrections of Germinal and Prairial
Oct.   Dissolution of the Convention—France ruled until 1799 by the
             Directory

1796
May   Conspiracy of the Babouvists

1797
Sept.   Republican *coup d'état* of Fructidor

1799
Nov.   *Coup d'état* of Brumaire—Napoleon Bonaparte seizes power

1800
Feb.   Creation of the Bank of France

1801
July   Concordat signed between France and the Papacy

1802
March   Peace of Amiens with Great Britain—hostilities resumed in 1803
May   Napoleon made Consul for life

1804
Feb.   Discovery of royalist plot, led by Cadoudal, on Napoleon's life
March   Completion of the Civil Code, renamed the Napoleonic Code in
             1807
May   Napoleon declared Emperor
Dec.   Napoleon crowns himself in Notre-Dame

1805
Oct.   Battle of Trafalgar
Dec.   Battle of Austerlitz

1806
Oct.   Battles of Jena and Auerstädt

1807
July   Treaty of Tilsit with Russia

1808
Sept.   Organisation of the Imperial University

1809
July   Battle of Wagram

1810
April   Napoleon's marriage to Marie-Louise of Austria

1812
June   Napoleon invades Russia

1814
April   Abdication of Napoleon—First Bourbon Restoration

1815
March   Napoleon escapes from the island of Elba and lands in the South
             of France—the 'Hundred Days'
June   Battle of Waterloo—Second Bourbon Restoration

Further Reading

The best contemporary accounts of social life in France during this period are given in Vidocq's *Memoirs*, Rétif de la Bretonne's *Les Nuits de Paris* and L. S. Mercier's *Tableaux de Paris*.

M. Baldet, *La Vie Quotidienne dans les Armées de Napoléon* (Hachette, 1964).

R. C. Cobb, *Police and the People* (Clarendon Press, 1970)

A. Cobban, *The Social Interpretation of the French Revolution* (C.U.P. 1964)

M. Carlson, *The Theatre during the French Revolution* (Cornell U.P., 1966)

N. Hampson, *A Social History of the French Revolution* (Routledge and Kegan Paul, 1966)

The First European Revolution (Thames and Hudson, 1970)

G. Lefebvre, *The Coming of the French Revolution* (Princeton U.P., 1967)

Napoléon (Peuples et Civilisations)

F. Markham, *Napoleon* (Mentor Books, 1966)

J. McManners, *The French Revolution and the Church* (S.P.C.K., 1969)

J. Robiquet, *Daily Life in France at the Time of the Revolution* (Allen and Unwin, 1962)

La Vie Quotidienne au temps de Napoleon (Hachette, 1946)

G. Rudé, *The Crowd in the French Revolution* (Oxford Paperbacks, 1967)

Revolutionary Europe (Fontana Paperbacks, 1964)

A. Soboul, *The Parisian Sans-culottes and the French Revolution* (Clarendon Press, 1964)

Index